What Pastors and Leaders Are Saying

"Dick Hardy has an intuitive genius for addressing the real-world issues that pastors grapple with. Dick's experience as both practitioner and consultant makes Right Turns an intensely practical, no nonsense guide for taking local church ministry to the next level."

Dr. James Bradford, General Secretary
General Council of the Assemblies of God Springfield, Missouri

"Most of us have questions, questions, questions. Dick has made it his priority to get answers, answers, answers. His greatest asset lies in his ability to guide questioners like you and me to answers that actually help. In Right Turns Dick consolidates his years of ministry experience and presents to us the most essential and practical elements of the wisdom he's gained. Get it. Read it. Do it. Your life and ministry will be forever enhanced."

Chris Mavity, Executive Director
North Coast Training
Vista, California

"If you need help navigating the leadership journey in the local church, there's nobody I'd recommend as a guide more than Dick Hardy. Dick can help you make the Right Turns you need to make to get to your destination!"

Glenn Reynolds, Lead Pastor
Bethel Church
Hampton, Virginia

D1069335

"Dick Hardy has been a coach, consultant and friend. The principles that he shares in his book, Right Turns will help every pastor, staff and church leader to begin to make good decisions. Dick's advice is practical, relevant and works in the real church today. I highly recommend this book for leaders who want their church to take the Right Turns."

Ron Squibb, Lead Pastor
International Christian Center
Staten Island, New York

"I love the way Dick Hardy tackles subjects everyone deals with but rarely talks about. He gets right down where the rubber meets the road, right where we all live and lights up the way."

Dan Berry, Lead Pastor
Cornerstone Church
Des Moines, Iowa

"I had the privilege of serving at a great church with Dick for over 15 years. He is a godly man whose writing is practical, motivational and Biblical. You want to read and share Right Turns."

John Palmer, President
Emerge Ministries
Akron, Ohio

"In Right Turns Dick exercises his uncanny ability to get into the collective mind of church leaders, address their most significant challenges, and offer solid coaching. This book is a tremendous blend of the conceptual and the practical."

Chad Harvey, Lead Pastor
Raleigh First Assembly
Raleigh, North Carolina

"Dick Hardy's Right Turns is the book I will turn to for the rest of my ministry as I seek to grow in my ability to serve my King and to encourage younger leaders. I will use it to challenge myself and to develop staff, elders, and other key leaders. Every section is chock full of practical wisdom, but Section 5 on staffing could not have arrived at a better time for me. Thanks, Dick, for being a friend to pastors and to the churches they lead!"

Hosea Bilyeu, Senior Pastor
Ridgecrest Baptist Church
Springfield, Missouri

"Insightful and very well written, this is a must read for any church leader looking to make their church a soul saving station."

Mark Shackelford, Chairman of Deacons
Lenexa Baptist Church
Lenexa, Kansas

"After reading Dick's first book, 27 Tough Questions Pastors Ask, I couldn't wait to read Right Turns. His insight to ministry is invaluable to those who want to further the impact of their church and effectively reach their community with God's love."

Charlie Salmon, Lead Pastor
Church on the Ridge
Snoqualmie, Washington

"Some books leave you with great concepts; others with the practical aspects of how-to. Right Turns does both."

Kendall Bridges, Lead Pastor
Freedom Life Church
Carrollton, Texas

"What I love about what Dick Hardy writes is when you get done you say, 'Yeah, I can do that.'"

Dary Northrop, Lead Pastor
Timberline Church
Fort Collins, Colorado

"You can pick up lots of church leadership books on theory or you can get one that hits the practics. Right Turns is that book."

Scott Wilson, Senior Pastor
The Oaks Fellowship
Dallas, Texas

"Dick Hardy has provided pivotal insight and guidance to me and my staff. As I returned to pastor my home church, his Right Turns aided us in our transition. This book is a must read for any church leader navigating the dangerous waters of change."

Jamie Austin, Lead Pastor
Woodlake Church
Tulsa, Oklahoma

RIGHT TURNS

DICK HARDY

FOREWORD BY MARK BATTERSON

RIGHT TURNS

THE 30 | **NAVIGATIONAL DECISIONS**
LEADING PASTORS MAKE
IN GROWING THE CHURCH

TATE PUBLISHING
AND ENTERPRISES, LLC

Published by Tate Publishing & Enterprises, LLC
127 E. Trade Center Terrace | Mustang, Oklahoma 73064 USA
1.888.361.9473 | www.tatepublishing.com

Tate Publishing is committed to excellence in the publishing industry. The company reflects the philosophy established by the founders, based on Psalm 68:11,
"The Lord gave the word and great was the company of those who published it."

Book design copyright © 2013 by Tate Publishing, LLC. All rights reserved.
Cover design by Jan Sunday Quilaquil
Interior design by Mary Jean Archival

Published in the United States of America

ISBN: 978-1-62510-279-9
1. Religion / General
2. Religion / Christian Church / Leadership
13.04.05

DEDICATION

To the woman who gave birth to me, I rise up this day to call her blessed—my mom, Donna Mae Hardy (1932–2008).

ACKNOWLEDGMENT

To many I give thanks for the inspiration they have been in the journey of writing *Right Turns*. The wonderful clients for whom I have the privilege of serving I can't say thanks enough. These churches and pastors serve as inspirations to me in communicating to others their best practices.

The lives of men like Jamie Austin, Merwin Pickney, Glenn Reynolds, Chad Harvey, and Tony Baker illustrate there are great men leading great churches. They are all different in age, experience, and station in life. They are all the same in demonstrating an unyielding determination to see people step across the line of faith and experience Jesus.

Thank you's go to Gary Brothers, Brian Ross, Charlie Tuttle, David Crispin, Rick Gannon, Henry Cloud, Craig Moore, Doug Lowery, Chris Mavity and Chad Harvey for their valued contribution to portions of the book.

Jonathan Hardy and his lovely wife Ashley are heroes to me in how they have launched the next generation of Hardys. I am proud of them both and Emery, the first granddaughter they gave us.

Caleb Masterson married the best daughter a man could ask for in mine, Erin Hardy Masterson. I love them for many things not the least of which is their gift to our family—our first grandson, Reid.

Pat, how could I ever navigate life without you? I couldn't. You have walked with me in all seasons of life and continue to do so today with a love for me far greater than I deserve. Thank you for believing in me and in our role to help pastors. I love you more than the ink on this page can say.

And finally, to the one who gives me eternal life, I thank you. Words cannot express the depth of my gratitude for your forgiveness of my sin and for your grace you have bestowed upon me. It is my prayer you will help me continue on the journey, impacting as many as you bring my way. I thank my God and savior, Jesus Christ.

CONTENTS

Dedication 9

Acknowledgment.. 11

Introduction.. 17

Foreword.. 19

Section 1   Leadership 21

1. Twenty-Two Observations of Lead Pastors of
    Larger, Growing Churches............................ 22

2. Responding to Tithe Terrorists 28

3. The Vision Is Not For Sale............................ 34

4. Aren't Prayer Meetings
    Kind of Old School? 39

5. Building a Culture of Continual Improvement
    Part 1 46

6. Building a Culture of Continual Improvement
    Part 2 53

7. Nine Thoughts on Ending Dead
    and Dying Ministries.................................... 60

8. Six Steps in Determining Which Ministries to
    Stop Doing 66

Section 2   Volunteer Development 71

   9.   Seven Thoughts on Recruiting Volunteers 72

  10. Four Aspects of Training Volunteers 76

  11. Eight Thoughts on Retaining Volunteers 80

Section 3   Guest Retention 85

  12. Thoughts on How to Retain Guests
      Who Visit Your Church Part 1 86

  13. Thoughts on How to Retain Guests
      Who Visit Your Church Part 2 90

  14. Why Don't Guests Come Back to Our
      Church? 94

Section 4   Personal Life 99

  15. Pastor's Personal Character 100

  16. Why Should a Pastor Have a Large Network of
      Friends? 107

  17. I'm not Good Enough or Smart Enough 112

  18. I'm Worn Out: What Do I Do? 115

  19. Seven Observations for Sabbatical Rest 119

Section 5   Staffing 125

  20. Thirteen Nonnegotiables between
      Lead and Staff Pastors 126

  21. Ten Thoughts for Lead Pastors in Leading
      Their Music/Worship Pastors 130

  22. Ten Thoughts for Music/Worship Pastors in
      Serving Their Lead Pastors 136

23. Five Reasons Second-Chair Leaders
    Lift First-Chair Leaders 142

24. Five Ways to Help Your Staff Pastor Grow in
    Effectiveness 147

25. Motivating a Pastoral Staff for Effective
    Ministry 152

26. Dealing with Staff Pastors Who Think They
    Are God's Gift to Everyone 160

27. What I Wish My Staff Members
    Understood 165

Section 6   Criticism 169

28. Six Things I Learned about Criticism 170

29. Nine Thoughts on Dealing with
    Founded Criticism 174

30. Ten Thoughts on Dealing with Critics Who
    Are Absolutely Clueless 178

INTRODUCTION

Questions abound for all church leaders. Of the volumes written on church leadership, many are theoretical in nature. *Right Turns* is not. This sequel to Dick Hardy's inaugural book, *27 Tough Questions Pastors Ask* deals with the nuts and bolts of ministry. It is practical and spiritual at the same time.

The author addresses six general categories of pastoral leadership: leadership, volunteer development, guest retention, personal life, staffing, and criticism. Each category is broken down into topics of significance to the local pastor.

This book's unique contribution to the church world is that it is written by a practitioner, not a theoretician. It is not written by a "preaching" pastor but one who has spent his life in ministry, walking alongside the lead pastors of two megachurches and a vice president of a denominational Bible college. The book is a step-by-step spiritual process guide.

A continual thread of the deep need for prayer and the commitment to the church's mission of reaching spiritually lost people with the gospel is woven throughout its pages. While many administrative personnel live with only the black-and-white bottom line, Dick Hardy lives with prayer and mission in continual focus. Each chapter's step-by-step process provides evidence of the importance of the book.

The stories relayed are real. The names of pastors, leaders, and churches, as well as their locations, have been changed. You are free to contact the author at www.thehardygroup.org to drill in further to circumstances you are facing where you might see outside help of value.

Right Turns purposes to be a pastor's and church leader's best friend, a spiritual nuts and bolts guide to navigating the twists and turns of ministry. This book provides the directions leading pastors choose in growing the church.

FOREWORD

In the life of a pastor, it doesn't take long to realize the preaching part of what they do is the fun stuff. Although lots of work, preaching and preparing to preach are some of the most enriching time in a pastor's week. It's all that other stuff they have to deal with that eats their lunch.

Dick Hardy has written literally a guide book on how to drill down on thirty decision points pastors confront. He has written at a level that is applicable to churches of all sizes. What I really appreciate about Dick's writing is he is clear that there are no templates to plop on one church from another. There are no formulas, no A + B = C. Each church has to navigate its own issues and come up with an approach that is specific to them. Dick talks about universal principles of doing church that transcend culture, location, and church size.

In addition, in my opinion, a book of this nature is of little value if it is not laced with the articulation of prayer's impact on all our decisions. Dick does just that. Throughout the book, he states to do this thing called church with God, anything is possible. To do church on your own, well, you're on your own.

I am excited you are taking this *Right Turns* journey. You and the church you serve will be better off for having done so. Make right decisions and watch God grow the church.

—Mark Batterson, Lead Pastor
National Community Church
Washington, DC
Author of *Circle Maker*

SECTION 1
LEADERSHIP

CHAPTER 1

TWENTY-TWO OBSERVATIONS OF LEAD PASTORS OF LARGER, GROWING CHURCHES

It was the end of a three-day weekend of consulting with a church I'd been aware of for most of my life. The lead pastor, Ric Schultz, had been in the saddle for right at a year. The staff had long preceded him. Ric had seen ministry done at a church of 1,100, and now in his first-time pastorate, he was leading a wonderful church of 550. His challenge? He knew what he wanted; to grow the church. But getting the staff to understand how it was going to look was his challenge.

It became clear to me while listening to the round-table discussion of these good staff members their picture of a church of 550. This was, in fact, a large church to them. However, this self-perception was slated to be a roadblock to that which Ric envisioned. Ric knew that in a metro area of 125,000, a church of 550 did not even scratch the service. I left that weekend meeting with a purpose to help Ric communicate what larger, growing churches look like and more specifically how lead pastors in those settings think.

While it is not true all lead pastors of all larger, growing churches are monolithic in their thinking or actions, I have observed twenty-two common traits of these leaders and the churches, staffs, and boards they serve. The following traits, in part, guide their leadership.

1. Lead pastors in these churches tend to put high demands on their staffs.

2. Staff pastors who thrive in these churches tend to be constantly changing what they do and how they do it.

3. Staff pastors in these cultures have to develop thick skins.

4. These churches are all about mission—reaching spiritually lost people with the gospel.

5. These churches have a strong focus on numbers. They believe every soul counts for eternity. What the leadership does to introduce people to God and disciple them in the faith is important enough to measure.

6. Lead pastors in these churches are intent on attaining and keeping unity. They do that through the strength and wisdom of their leadership. They do not capitulate to whiners.

7. These lead pastors generally understand they are in over their heads and have an extremely deep commitment to calling on God for their strength.

8. Staff pastors and board members understand where confidentiality starts and stops. If someone in the church wants to speak confidentially with a staff or board member and shares information that could be construed as working against the unity of the body or as harmful to the

body, the staff and board members understand their responsibility. That information has to be shared with the lead pastor, regardless of any confidentiality request. The individual needs to understand that position. No elements of disunity are allowed to ferment.

9. These lead pastors are seldom satisfied. Like Paul, they are content in the state they are in but understand that, until every person within their reach and influence knows Jesus, their work is not done. They tend to always be looking for ways to do everything better.

10. These lead pastors tend not to dwell on victory celebrations very long. They are regularly saying things like, "That was great. Now how can we do it better?"

11. Staff pastors frequently feel like they can never satisfy the lead pastor. While they work hard to perform, staff pastors like to celebrate wins for a longer period of time than lead pastors. Hence, they have the feeling they cannot satisfy their leader.

12. Lead pastors require staff pastors to be solution-oriented. There are not many things worse for a lead pastor of these churches than to hear a staff pastor say, "We tried that and it didn't work"— and then not offer a solution to the issue at hand. Staff pastors who cannot develop solutions do not last long at larger, growing churches.

13. Staff pastors can easily fall prey to the "My plate is already full" mentality, while the lead pastor says there is more to be done.

14. Lead and staff pastors with longevity in large church cultures have discovered the necessity of reinventing themselves. Those who do not find themselves and the church stagnating and/or out the door.

15. While not disregarding what longtime members of the church think or feel, lead pastors in these cultures make their decisions based on what is going to reach more people outside the walls of the church—as opposed to keeping those inside the walls of the church satisfied. They regularly teach and preach to those inside about the mission to reach those outside.

16. Lead pastors at larger, growing churches seem to be able to live with fewer people "liking" them than pastors of smaller churches. Regardless of how people feel about them, they make tough decisions and live by them.

17. Lead pastors of these churches are sometimes wrong but never in doubt.

18. Larger, growing churches are completely staff-led and board-advised.

19. No lead or staff pastor gets comfortable in larger, growing churches. When they do, the church stops growing.

20. Lead pastors continually look for newer, younger, fresher ideas to reach the demographic, most likely to make a life change for Jesus, the under-forty crowd. When this happens, older staff pastors who frequently reinvent themselves thrive.

21. Suggestions made by lead pastors of larger, growing churches often are not suggestions. If a peer makes a suggestion, staff pastors may consider the idea. If a lead pastor makes a suggestion, staff pastors may be well advised to consider the suggestion much stronger than when someone else makes the suggestion. Staff pastors either gain clarity from the lead pastor as to how strong they feel about their "suggestion," or they go ahead with the lead pastor's suggestion as an instruction of what the lead pastor really wants done.

22. Larger, growing churches and the pastors who lead them never read unsigned notes, cards, or letters. They do the same with e-mails under bogus names. They have no compulsion to respond to spurious attacks on character or actions of anyone if it is unsigned. Admins of these pastors know to throw those away without telling the pastor they came in. These gutless, unsigned communiqués are a blight on the Body of Christ, and these lead pastors never respond to them. Ever!

Let me give a caution to any pastor who reads these 22 traits and say, "I'm going to be this way because I want to pastor a larger, growing church." Slow down! You need to grow into the traits God wants for you *after* you pray and discern the wise course of action in reinventing yourself. To do otherwise will not serve you or the church well. In fact, it could be disastrous.

On that note, this list is not deemed to be the be-all and end-all so one could become a lead pastor of a larger, growing church. However, it is a starting place for those who are looking to move from where they are to where they believe God wants to take them—and the church.

CHAPTER 2

RESPONDING TO TITHE TERRORISTS

" I don't like what the church is doing these days, and you need to remember we are the ones paying the bill around here." Ever heard that one from a church member? If you haven't, sooner or later, it's going to happen. A wonderful saint, acting not so saintly, will challenge you with their giving. They suggest if you don't do things their way, they are going to stop giving and maybe leave the church. I call them tithe terrorists. They attempt to highjack the vision of the church and hold it hostage to their demands.

Pastor Greg Urton had been pastoring the formerly great and now in comeback-mode Riverdale Church in Oregon for the past twelve years. He and his wife, Erin, had moved out west from Iowa to pick up the pieces of a seventy-year-old former denominational church that fifteen years earlier had gone independent. Twenty-eight people attended the day the Urtons were voted in as pastors. By the time Greg and I were engaged in the consulting relationship, the church was consistently over five hundred and clearly on the upswing.

With all churches, there are those in the congregation who think they have influence beyond the norm. Greg came face-to-face with it last spring. The church leadership's excitement for the vision Greg had laid out to them in their annual January retreat began to explode. They unveiled the vision to the church body and moved forward with anticipation. Music was part of that vision.

Walter, was a grandfatherly member of the church for fifty-four-years and a long-time friend of Greg's. However, he began to express his disappointment with the direction being taken in dramatically turning the music to the guitar-driven, highly contemporary music.

Then retired insurance executive, Walter went where no pastor wants to go. "You know, Pastor, if this music thing doesn't get fixed, I and a number of people our age may need to consider going elsewhere. You know almost everyone in Prime Timers gives 10 percent and then some. Besides, most of the church's support for missionaries comes from our group. I'm don't think this is the direction the church wants to go. In short, you know I love you, Pastor, but either the music goes or me and my money go, and that probably goes for a bunch of us."

I had a thirty-five-year-old client pastor of a church of 850 tell me an older gentleman in the church told him, "You had better start wearing a tie in the pulpit, or I am going to take my tithes elsewhere." He ultimately left and a few months later died. What a sad way to end a Christian life.

Another client pastor of a church of 1,400 had an elder (in title, not in age) suggest to him if the changes the pastor was making didn't slow down, he would need to leave the church. The implication was that financially this would cause a hardship on the church. He left, and the church kept growing.

Lead pastors should not be thrown off balance when this happens. We are in the business of helping the church to be successful in fulfilling the mission God has given us to reach spiritually lost people. In doing so, there are times when our decisions and our actions cause a stir with some constituencies of the church. When this happens, lead pastors cannot be held hostage by wrongly motivated donors.

One kind of person who throws this threat up to a pastor is an older person. Please note, the vast majority of older people are thrilled the church is doing all it can to reach people. But every so often, you'll get a cranky one who believes it is older people with their accumulated resources who pay the bills. They believe younger people do not. Therefore they question why churches do so much to reach younger families, the ones who are not paying the bills in their minds.

The second kind of person is a person of means or one who gives largely. Again, please note, the vast majority of people of means and large givers are not this way. However, some have a distorted view of why they give. In these cases, they give to have influence, power, and control. All are wrong motives.

I find tithe terrorists almost always have an inflated view of their financial value to the church. The older tithe terrorist believes older people always give more. They often do, but this person also misses the understanding there are new generations of church leaders growing in their own careers, making money, and giving just as sacrificially. The person of means will frequently have ego issues that become manifest in this area.

While both types of tithe terrorists are of value to the church, the lead pastor cannot allow the self-determined overstatement of their own value to cloud decisions relative to the vision and direction of the church.

I've not met any pastor who is willy-nilly telling tithe terrorists to not let the door hit them on the way out. Churches don't seem to be overly flush with cash. Donors are important to accomplishing the church's mission. So how does a pastor handle this effort by some to hold the church hostage to their demands?

1. *Pray.* Generally we love these folks and want the best for them. However, what we can do for them on our own pales in comparison to what God can do. He will give you the wisdom and direction you need to navigate this in salvaging every misdirected person you can. At the same time, he is the one that keeps us on track to mission. You will hear his voice in prayer.

2. *Communicate.* Failing to be clear on the mission of the church is not acceptable. Lead pastors must regularly communicate from the pulpit the value of tithing and why we do it. Clearly articulate the instruction of the Word. When talking directly with the person, do the following:
   • State the church's position on vision.
   • State the church's position on giving.
   • State that you value the person.

- Ask them to restate what they think you just said.

3. *Be open in financial reporting.* You are asking for more tithe terrorists if you hide or gloss over the books of the church. Be open and clear in your reporting. You are not doing so for the church to vote on every little purchase of paper clips, but you are sending a message the church is a good steward of the resources given to it.

4. *Be calm.* Never engage a tithe terrorist in anger. Listen with intent to understand. Avoid the smart-aleck response I gave one of these folks once. "You gave the church the money, and the church gave you a tax deductible receipt. So we're even. Now what's your beef?"

5. *Be direct.* Avoid the temptation to dance around the subject. Help the person understand the vision of the church is not for sale. Help them know you value their presence at the church and are grateful for their faithfulness in giving back to the Lord his tithes. At the same time, make it clear giving does not buy influence.

6. *Bend without breaking.* If there are areas where you can bend on an issue with one of these folks, then by all means do so. There is nothing that says you can't bend from time to time. However, don't break. Please note that normally the demands of these folks are so off base that, in these cases, you don't negotiate with terrorists.

7. *Stand firm.* Be confident in what God has called
    you to do and to be. Understand standing firm
    is not being bullheaded or stubborn. It is stating
    and defending that which God has given you
    for the church. Stand firm.

In short, the vision God has given you cannot be held
hostage. Period. Please understand the vast majority
of your church members loves to give and does so out
of obedience and love for God. At the end of the day,
dealing with the very small number of tithe terrorists
who rear their heads in control every few years is part
of the lay of the land.

If nothing of consequence is happening at the
church, you probably won't have many of these folks. If
it is happening, and if you are making necessary changes
to move the church forward to accomplish the mission,
then there will be occasions when you will confront this
issue. Follow the guidelines given above, and God will
honor your effort to be respectful of all people yet stay
true to the vision he has given you for the church.

The mission and vision of the church will not be
held hostage by tithe terrorists!

CHAPTER 3

THE VISION IS NOT FOR SALE

Pastor Jerry Moran knew what he had heard from God. This great church of 2,500 he served in Ohio knew that about Jerry as well. How could you not know? Jerry and his wife had faithfully served the church for seventeen years, and by now he had a bit of a track record—and a good one at that.

All was going great until that fateful Tuesday when Ben walked into Jerry's office. Ben was a highly successful investment broker. His firm had weathered the downturn in 2008 and was flying financially higher than ever before, their clients beating the market by wide margins month in and month out. Needless to say, Ben was doing well personally as well—so well that his giving was 5 percent of the church's total. Jerry was aware of a person giving at that level but not knowing specifically it was Ben. However, in a church of this size, it was anyone's guess who it was.

"You know, Jerry, I've always been behind you in the things you have done. God has set Beverly and me as a blessing to the church. I think you know that. However, this effort you are proposing to bring inner-city teens into our building and mix with our kids, that's just not going to work. I have a fourteen-year-old daughter, and I certainly don't want her in any close proximity to some sixteen-year-old kid from the hood. You know what I mean." Jerry again explained the reason the church was doing outreach in this way and asked for Ben to be on board with the church and most importantly to pray for these young people. Ben's response was, "I don't give the kind of money I give to the church to sit around and have you do this kind of thing. Either you drop this inner-city teen idea, or I drop my giving."

What is it with some people who think they can influence the pastor and the church with their giving? I mean, *really*. Do they think the vision God has placed in the heart of the lead pastor is for sale?

I have heard it from far more than one of my client churches. A wealthy individual in the church attempts to influence the church's direction with a threat related to their giving. It is also not uncommon to hear of an older person suggesting their giving level should give them the right to have their way on any number of issues.

Both have the mantra "Do it my way, or I will pull my money and maybe leave the church." Implied with this threat is the church really needs them and their money. Of course, everyone is needed, but not at the expense of the vision of the church. By the way, I find it interesting in the majority of cases, those who tout the high value of their giving to the church regularly overstate its dollar value. It's not as high as they think.

One of the great privileges of a lead pastor is to be the receiver of the vision of the church from God. While the mission for the church to reach spiritually lost people is generally clear to most, the vision of how that mission is going to be accomplished can take many forms. On occasion, there are those who think vision is up for grabs—and even for sale. It is not.

The wise and discerning lead pastor seeks the mind of the Lord for direction for the church. The equally wise and discerning lead pastor communicates the vision to leadership, not in a condescending or arrogant manner yet confidently and humbly. The vision clearly comes through the leader.

It is imperative the lead pastor clearly communicate the direction the church is pursuing, both to the paid and lay leadership. In turn, clear and passionate communication should go to the body as a whole. It should not be just the latest and greatest idea from the leader; rather, it must become part of the DNA of the church. Smart pastors take this communication process seriously as it has the capacity to make or break the vision.

Here's the rub. There are times the vision or direction charted runs afoul of a lay leader or church constituent. This should not cause alarm. If a vision is big enough, it will take time for everyone to come on board. However, some will ultimately not buy in. Concern of this nature gives the lead pastor the opportunity to bring clarity and sometimes adjust nuances that are ancillary to the vision. Please note this does nothing but strengthen the vision.

Although this is the exception and not the rule, sometimes people can feel because they give to the church, they have a right to determine the church's direction. Sometimes, depending on the church's governance structure, vision has to jump hoops to become reality. If this is your church, I would go to work on governance to get that fixed. This only slows down vision. You don't see vision in Scripture having to navigate a maze of committees to become reality.

Vision is given to the lead pastor. He is the conduit through which God gives direction to the church. I am not suggesting a dictatorship by the lead pastor, but I do suggest vision is not given to the body as a whole, rather to the leader. Paid and lay leadership respond together to the vision and begin the process of moving forward.

When a person tries to exert influence over the pastor or church leadership, they are not following the proper line of spiritual authority and accountability. When they attempt this assertion of influence with the level of their giving, real or perceived, they have stepped way over the line. This is an issue of control. They would not say it this way, but in reality, they want to buy the vision. They want control—which is not good.

The leader receives the vision, and it is not for sale. Again, I am not suggesting an autocratic approach to vision, but I am suggesting members of the church do not have any authority to influence vision because of their giving. To think they do indicates a misguided understanding of giving. It also exposes wrong motivation and an overly inflated view of self.

The church does not operate as the world does, where money buys influence. Lead pastors who allow parishioners to pay for influence set the course for church decline and ultimate demise. Lead pastors who stand up against "selling of the vision" give their churches the greatest chance to succeed and flourish. God is honored in doing so.

While someone may attempt it, never allow anyone to buy the vision of the church. Never allow anyone to control you or the church. Lead pastors should stand firm in what they know God has given them. It is God's vision, not the lead pastor's. As well, it is not the strong donor's vision. It is God's vision. Seek it. Hear it. Proclaim it. Protect it. Never sell it.

CHAPTER 4

AREN'T PRAYER MEETINGS KIND OF OLD SCHOOL?

When Michigan pastor Lou Majeske was asked whether their church possessed a culture of prayer, he looked at me like a deer in the headlights. "What do you mean? We pray." He gave me the response I get from over half of the lead pastors with whom I engage. It is almost as if Lou felt like I insulted him by asking the question. The reality is that virtually all churches pray. All pastors pray. However, few churches truly possess a culture of prayer.

When I asked Lou if the church had any regular time of gathering together to pray corporately, he rattled off the usual beginning-of-the-year prayer and fasting emphasis many churches do. Weekly, however, there was nothing except the periodic weekly ladies' Bible study and the monthly men's group where people prayed. Truth be told, those times were actually more fellowship and food than prayer. Another Michigan church told me they have a weekly all-church prayer meeting. When I asked him when they had the prayer meeting, he told me every Thursday afternoons at 2:00 p.m. Hmmmmm…not well attended, I would guess.

Prayer meetings are definitely old-school. So old they go all the way back to Noah and the family as they departed that safety vessel called the ark and built an altar to the Lord. So, yes, if you want to get technical, prayer meetings are really old-school.

Seldom is this question verbalized, but actions speak louder than our words. Pastors are constantly looking for the formula to help their church grow. When someone suggests they begin to develop a culture of prayer, some pastors readily say, "I'm all ears. Tell me how?" Others get offended, saying, "I am a man of prayer. Everyone knows I am a man of prayer. Why would you think I am not a man of prayer?" These pastors completely miss the point. It is not about whether the pastor is a man of prayer. It is about the need for the congregation to possess a culture of prayer.

The former religion writer for a major Midwest newspaper once said to me, after I visited a Willow Creek Leadership Conference, "I believe in whatever career field Bill Hybels had chosen to enter, he would have done it big, just like he has at Willow." I agreed. At the same time, Hybels and any other megachurch pastor know that even with their own God-given ability, they cannot lead their church anywhere near as well on their own as they can with a culture of prayer inculcating their efforts. A pastor-friend of mine has said, "If we pray, all things are possible. If we don't, all bets are off."

Let's be clear in this discussion. This question of whether prayer meetings are old-school or not and whether they work in the twenty-first century is about whether we feel it can work to do corporate prayer. My answer to you is that it can. This has nothing to do with whether you are a man or woman of prayer, although I hope you are. It is all about the corporate DNA of the body of believers at the church you serve.

Here is my observation. Most churches have prayer ministry. Most churches do not have a culture of prayer, which is in their DNA. So I recommend you do the eight things listed below and watch to see what God does in the body.

1. *Pray to seek the mind of the Lord for the church you serve.* This is first. I know for anyone to suggest they do not this would seem ludicrous. However, I cannot overstate this. Do not start some sort of prayer meeting because somebody else somewhere else in the country has done it and their church has grown. Certainly, do not do it because you read it in this book or on some website. Churches do grow when they pray, and I do hope you follow the advice of this chapter. In all cases, however, do these things because God tells you to do so. You must believe it all the way deep inside that God wants you to begin to build a culture of prayer at the great church you serve. If you do not hear from God on this one, then feel free to skip just starting another "prayer" ministry to go along with all the others few people attend. But keep seeking God.

2. *Set aside a regular, specific time for the body to pray together.* I recommend you find some time each week where the body is challenged to meet together to pray. Do not wait for some catastrophe to occur for you to pray. Pray

continually. Do not set this meeting at 2:00 p.m. on Thursdays, 7:00 p.m. on Fridays, 8:00 a.m. on Saturdays, or at a time when people are not already planning to be at church. If you do, you will be sorely disappointed with the turnout. Sunday or Wednesday nights are your best bet. Yes, I know the church is already busy then. Do you want this to be part of your DNA or not? Whatever you do, pick a time that says to the body, "I, as your lead pastor, see this as high value, and we, as the church, are prioritizing this time of prayer together."

3. *Teach on prayer at the prayer meeting.* The Bible is full of instruction on prayer. This is the place where many pastors stub their toe. You have to teach. When you do, it is critically important you do all you can to leave these two elements at the door: your denominational description of prayer and your history in prayer. You must teach the Bible. Teach people to pray. Show people how to pray. Call on people to read Scripture and then pray. Ask them to pray as Jesus prayed. Now that's a novel thought!

4. *Teach the Bible versus tradition.* It really does not make a lot of difference what your faith tradition has shown you about prayer, even if it is totally biblically correct. The fact that it is totally biblically correct is what matters, not that it is your tradition. Most churches— whether mainline, conservative, evangelical, Pentecostal or other—carry with them baggage

as to what their tradition teaches. In some cases, their tradition matches Scripture. In others, it is way off base. All the while, in virtually all persuasions, an examination of Scripture will shed light on your tradition and likely cause you to pray differently, in a more biblical manner. Teach the body to pray.

5. *Reframe old stereotypes.* You have all sorts of folks who have crazy ideas of what a prayer meeting looks like, and many of those ideas miss the mark in terms of a biblical model for praying. One of the best ways to reframe is to actually demonstrate what a prayer meeting looks like. In doing so, you must be fully in tune with what God has for that prayer time together. On a practical level, do all you can to change up the prayer meeting. Weave in elements of congregational prayer, singing, prayer for specific corporate needs, small-group prayer for the personal expression of needs, your teaching (always teach) on prayer, and then *pray*. Listen for God's leading, keep it moving, and stop to wait on him when you sense that need. Yes, you can even do announcements and take up the offering—but don't forget to pray!

6. *Coach leadership.* The team around you must be taught on prayer. Your key lay leaders and paid staff must understand your heart for the church to pray. They cannot be left to their own devises to come up with the understanding you have or

the need for regular corporate prayer. You must demonstrate regularly that your focus on prayer needs to run as a common thread through all leaders. This does not happen by osmosis. Teach and coach your leadership on prayer.

7. *Model prayer in your own life.* Be aware you cannot simply talk about prayer meetings and the need for them without prayer being an integral part of your own life. You should not wear prayer as some sort of spiritual badge. However, those closest to you must see that prayer is a part of your own DNA, just as you want it to be for the corporate culture called "the church you serve." Model prayer.

8. *Plan to go the distance.* I have heard this statement and find it amazing: "We tried the prayer thing, and it didn't work." Wow! That which the Lord told us to do did not work? Hmmmmm... never quit! I mean, *never quit!* Starting a prayer meeting is not for the faint of heart. This process will be years in the development. That is a good thing. If you could just start it up in April and have it purring right along by June, it would be more like a man-inspired, short-term program than a God-inspired, long-term adventure. Plan to go the distance.

As noted earlier, most churches have prayer ministry. Not near as many have a culture of prayer. Why don't you be different? Try the old-school method of having regularly scheduled prayer meetings for the church to pray.

At the end of the day, I strongly encourage you to do the eight things listed above. Get started with hearing the mind of the Lord. Then step out of the boat and pray. Call the body to prayer. Indicate to them now and for years to come a major part of the DNA of this church is prayer.

Prayer meetings—are they old-school? Yes, very much so, *and* they work better than ever today. If you do not have a regularly scheduled, once-a-week time where the body prays together, I implore you to start. As a pastor, seek God first and then determine his plan for your church in the area of corporate prayer. It will be one of the greatest endeavors of your ministry life, corporately teaching your people to pray and growing in prayer yourself.

CHAPTER 5

BUILDING A CULTURE OF CONTINUAL IMPROVEMENT PART 1

There's nothing like working with a church that thinks it has arrived. Whether 50; 500; or 5,000; there are some that are perfectly satisfied with their current attendance. So when I talked to Pastor Caleb Chutter about the whole concept of improvement, he asked, "What's wrong with us?"

For churches, the issue is less about what is wrong with them than it is how they could be better. Caleb's church in Birmingham, Alabama, was a solid church of 750 average attendance. He called me in because, while the church had grown from 50 to 750 in eleven years, it had now plateaued for four years, and that was personally disconcerting for him as a pastor.

While he personally had the understanding something was probably going to have to change, he had inculcated in the body of believers there in Birmingham that to change much would mean the church was heading down the slippery slope of theological liberalism. Never mind they were doing a bunch of things mediocre to good, but with almost nothing done very, very well, those things had to change.

A legitimate question for Caleb was, "Where do I start?" For him and for you, that is a great question. I do not have an exact statistic, but I would say you are over halfway home for having asked it. Most don't. You know, however, the church you serve deserves nothing but the best in ministry that reaches lost people with the gospel.

Let's start with the low-hanging fruit. It is always best to get a few wins under your belt before you tackle the big stuff. Let me caution you as you read down through this list. You will be tempted to say something like, "Well, we are already good on two of these, so let's work on the others." Here's my response to that: It makes no difference at all whether you are "already good" at anything. The fact is you can be better.

You will start with failure if you have any sense at all you already do "good" at anything. We are not talking about whether you are good or bad at any of these. We are talking about the fact that whatever you do, you can do it better. Even the best church in the country can be better. So if I were you, I'd pay attention to all of these and then some.

1. *Guest services.* Start with an inventory of greeters, ushers, information center volunteers, parking lot hosts, etc., and ask yourself, "What are some things they could do to be better?" This is where you must not rely on what you have known to be "good" from your history in this church or others.

   I would start this thought process at the entrance to your property. Why not? Most other churches in town don't do this, so why don't you? Then how about placing hospitality folks on the parking lot, on the sidewalk, at the doors to the building, at the doors to the auditorium, and then inside the auditorium? How about creating a guest reception area after service? This is where you have to make observations and then respond with a "what if."

- Our ushers seem to be primarily in their fifties, sixties, and seventies. What if we had ushers in their teens, twenties, thirties, forties, fifties, sixties, and seventies? What would have to happen for this to be reality?

- Our ushers take up the offering and count the people. What additional services could these great volunteers do to serve those in the auditorium?

- We have two sets of double doors as you enter our building. We have a greeter on each set. What if we had two greeters on each set? How could that happen?

- We do not have a place for guests to meet and gather information about the church after service. What if we did? What could that look like? Who would be the best kind of person to serve in this role of meeting new guests after service? When could we start this?

- Other?

2. *Preaching.* I know this is the ticklish one. Although all the other items in this list are very important, this is the one that can never be ignored. I am not suggesting in your desire to improve you continually beat yourself up over how bad you are. I am suggesting you take steps to evaluate

all pieces of your preparation, preaching, content, and delivery. I recommend you become a student of preaching. Take a video of yourself and ask a trusted friend to evaluate your message for timing, personal quirks, flow, etc.

Work to measure your words in a way their delivery has the most profound impact on the hearing. While you certainly must do the hard work of improvement, you must also immerse this effort in prayer. Without it, you will fall woefully short in your improvement. Ask these questions:

- I preached 35—40 minutes. What could I have deleted to preach 25—30 minutes and maintain all the salient points of the message?
- My body language did not seem to add to the message, or it seemed to be aimless. How could I make my body language augment what I am saying?
- What can I do to tighten all transition points?
- How can I improve my voice inflexion to improve the receipt of the message to the hearer?
- Other?

3. *Ministry to children.* How can you continually improve on ministry to children? First, recognize the world from which the children come. It is a media-saturated world. They come to your building on visual overload. You need to ask yourself, "How does what we do at church

compare to what they are exposed to during the week?" Do not fall prey to the "we don't have enough money to compete with that" mentality. You can improve. If you are doing what you did two years ago, you have fallen behind.

Always look for the latest and greatest because that is what the kids are exposed to. Then put in place all of the high values of the church spiritually, relationally, and physically. Your kids deserve the best. Ask yourself the question, "When moms are at Walmart and talking about the best children's ministry in town, how frequently will your church be in the mix?" It needs to be, and, no, it doesn't take zillions of dollars to be there. Step by step ask these questions:

- How do we train our teachers, and how could we do it better?
- What do our kids facilities look like, and how could we make them better?
- How do we measure whether our children are learning the Bible effectively? How can we improve our measurements, and how can we improve the children's learning?
- Other?

4. *Ministry in music/worship.* This early component of the worship service is the one that draws the body into the presence of God. It sets the stage for what is going to happen through the preaching of the Word. It touches the inner being of those

seeking to grow closer to God. When music is done well, it is best able to accomplish all of the above. When it is not, it not only shortchanges that which could be, but it is also potentially a hindrance to the positive response to the message on the heart of the pastor.

Working toward improvement in this area probably carries with it the greatest fear of being struck by lightning. The wonderful gifts of musicians to the church should never be discounted. At the same time, the temperament of those involved sometimes makes the insistence on "better" a too frequently personal matter. Given you have what you have in terms of musical talent, I would consider these thoughts and questions:

- Examine the quality of the musicians. How can you build a culture that assures each person you as the lead pastor want to enable them to improve?
- The music selection sometimes does not complement the sermon. How can you work better with the worship leader to ensure a seamless theme for each service?
- Our transitions are not tight. How can the worship team learn the importance of how their music is received in the minds and ears of the hearers?
- Other?

This should keep you going for a while.

By the way, after you have improved all the low-hanging fruit and gone onto the tougher issues at hand, what do you think you should do next? Go back to the top of the low-hanging-fruit list and do what? You've got it. Start all over again and watch how God will bring continuous improvement and increase to your ministry.

CHAPTER 6

BUILDING A CULTURE OF CONTINUAL IMPROVEMENT PART 2

Caleb was conservative. In fact, let's say Caleb was beyond conservative. There was much of what I saw at the church that was '80s with a touch of '90s and even some '70s. It was very nostalgic for me but a bit short on relevance to nonbelievers in Birmingham. Right after my first visit with him, the worship pastor of ten years resigned. This was the perfect opportunity for him to begin to make improvements in worship and at least get the church to 2000 with hopes he could get beyond 2010 within the next few years.

However, drilling down into further aspects of improvement began to make him very uncomfortable. Never mind it was already 2013. He felt like doing anything with Sunday school was tampering with his core values. When I suggested creating an environment attractive to young families, including creating a room or space for nursing moms, his sense was that would be catering to the consumer mentality of young adults. However, I will give Caleb credit. At the end of the day, he was able to see beyond the forms of doing church and began to see how improvement did not strike at doctrine. If the church was going to get better, Caleb realized the systems and thought processes he had in place had to change.

Certainly after a church has started down the road to building a culture of continuous improvement, it seems prudent to examine the very systems that got them to their current station in ministry. While the previous chapter addressed the more upfront and visible components of the church, this chapter is designed to move you forward in improving the infrastructure.

Remember, this is not about where you are on quality-of-infrastructure, 1–10 scale. This is about how you move one notch closer to 10 and beyond. You can be better at each of these four items listed below.

We like to think if we just have a razzle-dazzle service, the crowds will flock to it. Doesn't happen! I want you to start thinking about how you can improve each of the following four items. Be critical in your examination of every nuance of these four. Remember, this is not an exhaustive list, rather, a continuation of the process of improvement.

1. *Facility appearance.* This one can have as many opinions as zebras have stripes. You need to identify the person in church that is the most fastidious (perfect) in their attire and appearance of their home. Have that person do an inventory of your entire facility, inside and out. Do not put restrictions on their observations, things like, "Don't bother with the crumbling parking lot because we don't have money to fix it." That approach will shoot you in the foot. Then list everything in rank and order and go to work as far as your volunteer crew and budget will allow. You will improve. Questions for consideration are the following:

- I would rank our curb appeal at a 7 on a 1–10 scale. How can we make it an 8?
- If I were to compare our lobby to that of the finest high-end department store, I would say we are a bit over half as nice appearing as they are. How can we make it three-fourths as good as they are?
- The platform of our church is nice. How can it be neater and visually more appealing?
- Our nurseries are a busy place and tough to keep up with. What systems could we put in place to make them neater, cleaner, and more visually attractive?
- Are our walls throughout our building buff or white? Do you think we could upgrade to a cooler, newer look? Ya think?
- Other?

2. *Flow of service.* Depending on the style of your church, this can go all over the map. Here's the drill. If your church is so predictable you can set the oven timer for the roast by when the offering is taken in the service, you probably need to start mixing it up a bit. If your church is so loosey-goosey that nothing is predictable, you may want to tighten it up a bit. The point is you are trying to reach a market of people who are not attuned to whatever tradition of church you come from. You need to look at what you do from their eyes. There should be no wasted time

in a service as valuable as yours. Here are some questions to ask yourself:

- At the beginning of the service, does someone stand up from the platform and greet the folks? Why? Is there a reason to do this?
- Why do you pray for the offering?
- What can we double up on to save time?
- Do you meet and greet and for how long? If you were a guest and knew no one, is a five-minute meet and greet overkill?
- Does the church feel folksy? Is that good or bad for people who aren't part of the "folks"?
- Other?

I recommend putting a clock on every single piece of the service, including lengths of each song, transitions, length of each prayer, sermon length, announcements, everything. You might be surprised how you can streamline and increase your effectiveness, maybe improve.

3. *Guest follow-up.* One of the primary groups of people we follow up on is those who of their own accord visit the church. These people are generally in one of two camps. The first is the person or family who is new in town and looking for a church home. The other is someone in town who is unchurched or for whatever reason is looking for a new church home. How can you reach and touch these people better? Ask yourself these questions:

- What does a guest experience the minute they hit our property? How could that be better?
- What does a guest feel like when they leave our service? How could they feel better?
- Guests are told to fill out a guest card and/or to go back to the welcome center to pick up a gift from the church. How can the staff or volunteer leadership value the guest better than that? What could be done to make this piece of the guest visit more than just gathering their information?
- Our community's culture doesn't like to be contacted after a visit. What is the way to look at this postservice contact in a different light? How could we make contact that is palatable to the culture and sets our church apart from the standard expectation of guests who visit churches?
- Every church sends out thank-you letters to guests. What else could we do to touch them and increase their interest in returning?
- Other?

4. *New convert discipleship.* This is probably the struggle of most every pastor who is serious about reaching and retaining spiritually lost people. On one hand, it is always important to keep your expectations in check on how many people will actually follow through on a new commitment. On the other hand,

it is our responsibility to be as diligent as we can in creating systems that afford them that opportunity in the best possible way.

I suggest to churches the system for new convert discipleship you have in place is not near as important as working the system. Get the plan and work on it. The stakes could not be higher than on this one. Don't live in the frustration that when you preach the Word, people seem to respond, but then the church never grows. Pray, think, and act in the anticipation you can get better at retaining new converts. Ask these questions and more:

- What emotions does a new Christian experience when they walk back out of your building? What could we do to help them navigate those emotions?
- Responding to our appeals for salvation is easy. Does that affect commitment levels? Is there an inverse connection between ease of appeal and commitment? If there is, what could we do to make the appeal not quite so easy?
- Responding to our appeals for salvation is difficult. Does that affect commitment level to the positive? How can we make it easier to respond but not too easy?
- We do not ask anything from a new convert, i.e., next step is baptism, then membership, etc. How could we set in place the next immediate steps for them?

- The class we offer new converts following conversion is weak. How can we make it better?
- Our new-convert disciplers get discouraged. How can we provide better training for the long haul of discipling someone and for better end results?
- Other?

There you have it—facilities, flow of service, guest follow-up and new-convert discipleship. Each of these by themselves will produce results far beyond where you are currently. Collectively, they have the capacity to set your course on a new and improved path to reaching the mission of the church.

Don't forget. When you get them all whipped, start all over again!

CHAPTER 7

NINE THOUGHTS ON ENDING DEAD AND DYING MINISTRIES

Who in the world ever stops doing ministry? There's a leadership question for you. In most churches, they start ministries really well. But quit ministries? That would be tantamount to sinning. Jerry knew that to be the case in his Ohio church.

Jerry had been an administrative pastor at the church back in the day. When the lead pastor had to resign due to a moral failure, the board turned to thirty-three-year Pastor Jerry. In way over his head, Jerry began the process of examining every ministry to determine its relevance to then-current 1990. On paper, it was a wonderful concept. Do what works and ditch the rest. You know how that turned out.

I know at your church, all ministries continually flourish year after year, decade after decade. However, those other pastors out there like Jerry sometimes find themselves wondering what to do with the ministry Herb or Mabel started in 1973 that is no longer relevant or effective now.

Our churches have the privilege of doing ministry on a variety of fronts. We do so to meet the needs of the church and those who need to come to a relationship with Jesus. However, in doing so, we must evaluate the current effectiveness of all we do. Our methods of accomplishing the mission of the church must regularly

come under close scrutiny, or we can find ourselves
deluded into believing our bundle of activity is actually
effective when it probably is not.

Most churches are great at starting ministries
and deplorable at ending them. Somehow we have
convinced ourselves ending a ministry is unspiritual.
The ministry had a good reason for starting, so it must
have a good reason for continuing. Never mind the fact
the reason for starting may no longer exist.

Here are some thoughts for your consideration in
stopping some ministries in order to advance others:

1. *Pray first, not last.* When heading into the ending
    of a ministry that has served effectively for its
    time and is no longer, a leader must pray, pray,
    and pray again. To not do so can certainly cause
    much confusion, hurt, and chaos. Do not pray
    as a last resort. It is your first resort. It will pave
    the way for the best discontinuance and most
    effective movement to a new high-value focus.

2. *Strong leadership.* In order for ministries to end,
    the lead pastor of the church must be strong
    in their own leadership. This is not to say they
    should be a dictator. It is to say they must have
    a security and strength within them to chart the
    course and stay at it when the wind of resistance
    rears its head. Confident leadership sometimes
    eludes lead pastors, but it need not. They can be
    confident in their calling from God to serve their
    local church. A pastor can rest in the confidence
    of having prayed and done his or her homework

in the anticipation of the ramifications of ending a ministry. Never should the pastor assume that just because they say a ministry needs to end, it will do so without the gnashing of teeth. Strong leadership prepares for all potential outcomes, including the loss of some people who are unable to accept the change.

3. *Culture of change.* Change happens with the right people in place. The leader must be a continual student of change. The culture of change must be taught, taught, and retaught at every stage in the life of the church. This is a months-and years-long process. Pastors who want to move their congregations forward in attaining their mission will always talk about change and the necessity of it. To do otherwise will destine the church to carrying the dead weight of ministries that have long since lost their effectiveness. This drains the ability of the church to focus on those ministries that are of the highest value and impact.

4. *Pruning.* This is where it really happens. In order for a plant to grow and flourish, it must be pruned. Dr. Henry Cloud wrote an outstanding book *Necessary Endings: The Employees, Businesses, and Relationships That All of Us Have to Give Up in Order to Move Forward.* In it he notes pruning entails cutting off three different kinds of buds and branches: dead branches that take up space, sick branches that are not going

to get well, and healthy buds or branches that are not the best ones.

Putting it in church ministry terms, a pastor must ask, "Are there ministries at our church that are dead, not producing anything living? Are there ministries that are sick and are not likely to get well?" The answers to those that end in pruning can make sense to a lot of people. However, the question, "Are there healthy buds that are not the best buds?" and the potential to prune these is much more difficult to navigate in the church.

The reality is without cutting off those ministries, the very best buds on the best branches will be stymied in their ability to be as effective to mission as they can be. Pruning is painful, but it must be done to have the very best plant and the very best ministry.

5. *Hoping versus wishing.* Dr. Cloud asks the question every lead pastor asks, "What is worth keeping and fixing, and what should end?" We all hope a ministry that has slipped can come back. Everybody loves a comeback kid. For those ministries that have emanated out of the heart of a valued volunteer and have slipped, become stagnate, or have died, a comeback is sometimes wishful thinking. Wishing a ministry can be what it was seldom works. However, hoping a ministry can be what it was is possible when these nine objective factors from Dr. Cloud are in place.

- Verifiable involvement in a proven change process
- Additional structure
- Monitoring systems
- New experiences and skills
- Self-sustaining motivation
- Admission of need
- The presence of support
- Skilled help
- Some success

If all you do is wish for a ministry to be revived, you are only prolonging the inevitable of having to give it a burial or having to continue with an anemic church with strong ministries being diminished because of the drain of weak ones.

So what are the steps a lead pastor should take when ending a ministry? Here are a few basics:

- Pray. God birthed the ministry. He can take it home.
- Talk to key leaders. Don't be rash. Be thoughtful. Take the time necessary to bring as many people along with you in the understanding of the need to take action. Understand not everyone may make the journey with you. Help all involved understand our message never changes, but our methods to communicate it change all the time.
- Don't make a public spectacle of a discontinuance of ministry unless it has to be done. Be

noisy about the start of ministries. Be quiet about their funerals.

- Focus on the future.

The future is too important to be hamstrung with ineffective ministries. Some successful ministries of the past have become a hindrance to the future. If it were easy to stop doing those ministries, then every church would do so. But it is not. Therefore, it is your role to help guide the church to discontinuing some good things in order to do the best things. Your mission is too important to do otherwise.

CHAPTER 8

SIX STEPS IN DETERMINING WHICH MINISTRIES TO STOP DOING

One of the great personal strengths Jerry brought to the table was his administrative background and analytical thinking. Some did not always view those gifts as very spiritual, but they sure came in handy when he started the process of determining which ministries to keep and which to stop doing.

In Jerry's case, he gathered in as many key leaders as possible and began to give critical analysis to how successful each ministry was to the mission of the church. He used a process similar to what I will describe to you in this chapter. While it is not a be-all and end-all, at least for Jerry and this Ohio church it helped them minimize the collateral fallout of discontinuing ministries that used to be highly effective but whose time had long since passed.

When a pastor surveys the landscape of the church, they normally see a plethora of wonderful ministries that are truly effective in fulfilling the mission of the church. However, there are times when a pastor suspects an effective ministry of the past may have seen its best days, may be on the decline, and should probably end. The question that comes into focus is, "How does one know for sure?"

The lead pastor must always maintain the role as the leader in decisions that have to do with the various and sundry ministries of the church. While holding to that position, I recommend the lead pastor and the church go through the following process to determine whether to discontinue a ministry. This is not a casual six-minute process. This will be an intensive evaluation of activities with deep spiritual roots. It should not be taken lightly. It is best done according to the collective wisdom of the church leaders and staff.

1. *Determine the core mission of the church.* You do not need to look much farther than Matthew 28:19–20a, (esv): "Go therefore and make disciples of all nations, baptizing them in the name of the Father and of the Son and of the Holy Spirit, teaching them to observe all that I have commanded you." Without this mission, the church has no reason to exist. Make sure before you start any process of evaluation you have this standard clearly embedded in people's minds. You do not need a shifting measure while you are trying to determine the effectiveness of a ministry. You need a clearly identified core mission of the church. If you do not do this one right, you are set up for big problems down the line.

2. *Create a list of key leaders.* Determine which people you want to participate in the evaluation of ministries. These should generally be staff and board members, not the whole church. They could be key ministry leaders as well. However, just be careful you do not set up a

system whereby one ministry leader tries to beef up their ministry to the detriment of another. Inherent in this process will be a sense of defensiveness when it comes to pet ministries. Please be careful with those you choose for evaluators. When possible, I recommend only using board and staff. For illustrative purposes only, let's assume you choose nine leaders.

3. *List all ministries.* Have everyone in leadership list all conceivable ministries of the church. Do not just list children, youth, and adult ministries. List the various ministries within each of them and every other ministry. By the time you are done with this list, it will probably be fairly lengthy. Do not gloss over anything you are doing in ministry by not including it. For illustrative purposes only, let's assume an arbitrary number of sixty-two ministries.

4. *Rank all ministries.* This will be very time consuming. Have your key leadership of nine people rank all the ministries from top to bottom in effectiveness to reaching the core mission of the church, not by how much they like the ministry or the people in it. It is all about core mission. In our illustration of sixty-two ministries, all nine leaders must rank them 1 (most effective to mission) to 62 (least effective to mission). This means in the middle of the pack, they will have to make a personal determination that, for example, ministry number 24 is more

effective than ministry number 25 and less effective than ministry number 23. Yes, I know it will be tedious, but it is necessary to gaining a collective agreement as to which ministries are most effective to mission and which are least effective to mission.

5. *Calculate a collective ranking of the ministries.* For example, if you have nine leaders doing this collective ranking, you should add the numbers together of all sixty-two ministries as ranked by the nine leaders. I recommend throwing out the high and the low rankings of each ministry. That way, for example, if eight of the nine leaders felt the ABC ministry was ranked either as number 3 or number 4 and the ninth person ranked it number 61, the ninth person skews its ranking. Removing the high and the low mitigates this issue. Take the collective ranking of all ministries and list them in rank order with the smallest number at the top and the largest at the bottom. The small-number rankings are more effective-to-mission ministries. The large-number rankings are less effective-to-mission ministries.

6. *Begin to systematically discontinue the bottom 10 percent of ministries.* In our illustration of sixty-two ministries, this would mean the bottom six ministries would be up for discussion to set dates to discontinue them. At all times, while listening to the collective wisdom of the leaders, the lead pastor must remain the decision-

making leader. People will begin to provide a number of reasons to keep these ministries, but none will drive to the core mission of the church. They will almost always have to do with the nice people who work in those ministries and the concern for their feelings. If you are diligent in following this process, you will be positioned best to stay true to the collective evaluation of your leaders. If you end these six ministries, your core mission will not be affected in the least, and you will gain energy to put toward the top six ministries. Once this process is completed, you can go on to the next 10 percent until you have refined the effectiveness of your ministries and are investing the best of your energies in that which will drive to your core mission.

I do not pretend to suggest this is simply a nuts and bolts, easy-to-implement process. I do suggest it is necessary if you are going to stop doing the less effective ministries—those that are preventing you from doing the most effective ministries that drive to your core mission. Is it clear to you now why the articulation of core mission is so important? It is critical to the long-term focus of your church.

SECTION 2
VOLUNTEER DEVELOPMENT

CHAPTER 9
SEVEN THOUGHTS ON RECRUITING VOLUNTEERS

One of the things I learned early on in working with Pastor Greg was the high value he placed on volunteers. He did not see them as many pastors do as people to plug slots on the chart or worse yet to do so with the revolving door of the fifth-grade boys Sunday school class. Greg knew volunteers were the bread and butter of ministry. Greg knew if the church was going to move past twenty members twelve years ago and past five hundred today, he needed to recruit some of the best people with giftings to fit critical roles of ministry.

Ever heard these? "We have more volunteers than we know what to do with." "We don't have enough rockers in our nurseries for all the volunteers." "We've had to tell junior-high adult workers some of them have to go home because there aren't enough kids for their supervision."

Probably not. Neither did Greg.

Why not? Because in the world of church, there always seems to be more to do and not enough workers to get it done.

Let's think about this. The mission we are about is the greatest on the planet: the opportunity to reach spiritually lost people with the gospel. That should be enough to generate all the workers ever needed. However, Jesus notes in Matthew 9:37, esv, "The harvest is plentiful, but the laborers are few." So rather than beat yourself up because you don't have enough volunteers, just acknowledge it is the lay of the land. Then get to work recruiting!

In doing so, here are some thoughts for consideration:

1. *Have value.* Ever been asked to do something and end up asking yourself, "Why in the world am I doing this? What's the point?" Pastor, you can never let that happen in your ministry. Everything you invest time in doing, whether high profile or low, must have value—and that value needs to be communicated to volunteers. Clean toilets have value not simply because you like clean porcelain but because those who use the toilets are also valuable to God and to you. Volunteers who clean them need to see this value.

2. *Ask rightly.* This becomes particularly acute when you are dealing with high-capacity volunteers. I remember once asking a high-capacity volunteer to hang a banner in a classroom. Could he do it? Not very well, because, although he told me he would do anything for the church, his gift set was in far different arenas than working with his hands. As far as I know, he never served the church again. I wasted the time and talent of a high-capacity volunteer because I did not ask rightly of him. Learn the gifts and talents of your volunteers before you ask. Then ask rightly of them to fit who they are.

3. *Ask largely.* People love challenges. Give them one! Learn the capacity of your volunteers and

direct them as high as they can go. Be sure not to confuse this with somehow creating a "high-class" and "low-class" volunteer system. It is not. The widow in Scripture is celebrated because she gave largely of her mite—the small portion she possessed. The multimillion-dollar businessperson would not be celebrated for their mite. Why? Because it would not be a large gift for them. As is true for treasures, the same is true for talent. Recruit to the largest capacity of your volunteers. They will be more fulfilled in what they do for the church, and the ministry will benefit.

4. *Cast big vision.* Who in the world wants to be part of something small and insignificant? There are certainly volunteers who have no interest in being front and center on the main stage, but even the smallest of ministry-visible tasks needs to be tied to *big vision.* Cast it!

5. *Don't be phony—be real.* You need the toilet cleaned but don't create a disconnect by tying the task to something multiple separations away. Be real. Having a toilet cleaned by a volunteer does not correlate directly to a million dollars being raised for missions. So don't tell them that. However, without many clean toilets, it is almost certainly true the church won't raise a million dollars for missions—because people stop coming to places that don't have clean

toilets. Do tell them that. Don't be phony. Be real.

6. *Don't be desperate.* A buddy of mine, Chris Mavity of North Coast Training (www.northcoasttraining.org), noted to me it is critical the person (that would be you) asking a volunteer to join the team never be desperate. Whether you feel like it or not, you are not desperate. God has all the resources you need, and it is your job to systematically walk through the process of recruiting. If you feel desperate, don't show it. You'd better fake it 'til you make it!

7. *View recruiting as fun.* You may say, "This is not even close to fun." Then you either need to reframe what you are doing or get out of the business of ministry. The lifeblood of ministry is volunteers. Besides , I read someplace we are to be the equippers of the saints for goodness' sake—my paraphrase. Look at recruiting as a challenge and as fun!

So what do you think? Is it worth it? Are the good people under your care worthy of recruiting to the greatest mission on earth? You bet they are—and it is a high honor and privilege of yours to recruit them. In doing so, you provide fulfillment of the call of God on their lives, and you advance the ministry of the church.

CHAPTER 10

FOUR ASPECTS OF TRAINING VOLUNTEERS

Greg knew it is one thing to put the pitch on to a prospective volunteer, and it is completely something else to train them to be all they can be in the role you're asking of them. Greg's mantra became, "Train, train, and retrain. And when you're done, six months later, do it again." It had served him well over the last twelve years, and he was confident it would do so for the next twelve.

Training is everything! There is not much worse in the church than to put on the big push for volunteers; put your heart into communicating how badly volunteers are needed in the nursery, the junior-high ministry, or cleanup crew; and then *not train* them. Everybody loses when this happens.

My wife and I visited a restaurant the other day. It had a big write-up in the media, and so we thought, "Why not?" We went. Wow! Talk about a disappointment. Our only question upon leaving was related to how long they will stay in business. The servers and entire staff of the restaurant were so poorly trained. They had no idea what to do with people. Our meal tasted okay. Well, the meat was a little tough. The rolls never came. The drinks were refilled once. The dessert never came. The ticket never came. We never saw the server again. We asked another server for water and mustard. You guessed it. Neither came. A poorly trained staff was this restaurant's undoing in the end, about two months later.

When you have the high honor of working with people who give their time to the Lord, you as the pastor have the high responsibility to train them to be all they can be. Why would you do anything less? To this end, here are some recommendations for your consideration in training these high-value gifts from God.

1. *Never assume.* Simply because someone has said yes to your appeal does not mean they have anywhere near the understanding of what you really want. Never assume. If you assume because they've been around a long time or because the volunteer role is so simple they understand your expectations, you will more often than not be in for a rude awakening. Never assume. Always *presume* the volunteer knows nothing—not in a condescending way but in a cover-your-bases kind of way. When you presume they know nothing, then even if you explain something they already know or understand, you have the confidence no stone is being left unturned in terms of their understanding of what you expect to be done in their volunteer role. Never assume.

2. *Start with the basics.* After losing a football game back in the '60s, legendary football coach Vince Lombardi met with his team the next day for practice. To those Green Bay Packers, some of the greatest football athletes of that era, he held up the ball and said, "Gentlemen, this is a

football." It all starts with the basics. Games are won and lost on the fundamentals, the basics. In our world, try basics like prayer, discipleship, commitment, and reproduction.

3. *Teach the practics.* With any ministry, there are nuts and bolts of what has to happen and what should never happen. If the volunteer role is worth doing, write down what it is that is worth doing. Then do the well-worn drill: tell the volunteer what you are going to teach them, then teach them, then have them watch you do what you just taught them, then have them do what they watched you do while you watch them do it, and then let them go and do it by themselves. Finally, once the practics have been taught, always demonstrate proper leadership by regularly inspecting that which you have taught.

4. *End with the basics.* It's not that complicated. Whether it's a high-level or entry-level volunteer role at church, when you cut it all away, it's not that complicated. Stay basic. Stay fundamental. Razzle-dazzle doesn't win many football games, and it won't do so in church ministry either. End with the basics. When you pray, disciple, commit, and reproduce, good things will happen in an orderly way, and God will be honored. Remember, after you have trained a volunteer, it will be necessary to brush them up from time to time, to train in the basics all over again. Everyone wins when you do so.

When the best of the best perform, whether on the field, court, or stage, we see the end result of training, training, and more training. It doesn't happen overnight with them nor does it do so with your volunteers. Invest in them. Train them. Then watch as God does what only he can do with a volunteer surrendered to him and trained by you.

CHAPTER 11

EIGHT THOUGHTS ON RETAINING VOLUNTEERS

When I landed on site with Pastor Greg, he was in a period where volunteers were dropping like flies. He could not figure it out. He recruited like normal. He trained like normal. However, now he seemed to be refilling slots that had been previously held by long-term, committed volunteers. He told me he could not figure out while he was no longer retaining his volunteers.

There certainly wasn't an easy answer for that one. However, upon closer examination, we began to see some cracks of process that had become blind spots for Greg. Because he was good at recruiting, he began to take that for granted and started racing people through training, which was not his forte. In hindsight, he saw he was beginning to take those wonderful, long-term volunteers for granted and was not continually pouring into them.

When you go all the way back to the beginning of the process, you may be like Greg had become. Oh, the joys of recruiting a volunteer. The slots are filled, and you can rest easy. Oops! What happened? They quit. Ever experience that one?

We have all heard the stats on how much work it takes to gain the ministry services of a volunteer compared to how much work it takes (a lot less) to retain those same ministry services. Retaining is a whole lot easier, and it forgoes much of the angst of recruiting.

So what are some thoughts on retaining the gifts of people God gives us in our churches, those we call volunteers?

1. *Create teamwork.* There are not many lone rangers out there these days. The best volunteers perform in the context of a team. While there are certainly singular tasks that need to be done in ministry, the more that can be tied to a team, the better. It builds energy and enthusiasm. Further, it builds camaraderie and helps tie people together, thereby improving volunteer retention.

2. *Provide training.* There is not much worse than putting on the big recruiting pitch on Sunday morning and then sticking volunteers in slots without training. Your "org" chart will look good, but it will fall apart quickly. Do not recruit without a well-thought-through plan of how you will train, even for the simplest of ministry roles. The best of all people in all fields of endeavor train, train, and retrain. The high-value volunteers at the church should be no different.

3. *Resource adequately.* Few churches are overresourced, particularly in the area of money. However, there is no excuse for putting the time and effort of your volunteers on the front lines without providing them the resources to accomplish the task or ministry you desire from them. By the way, money is not the only resource. Your time investment in them is a resource. Supplies are resources. Continuing

education is a resource. You get the drift. Resource adequately.

4. *Expect commitment.* This can be the Achilles' heel for many of us in ministry. We whine and moan because of the low commitment levels of our volunteers. While it is true the younger generations coming onto the scene in ministry have vastly different views of what constitutes commitment, it is our role to set the bar high in terms of what we expect. If you expect little, you'll get little. Expect largely and more often than not you'll get it. Expect commitment; you'll get it, and you will retain more volunteers because of it.

5. *Maintain proper expectations.* This is one of the greatest challenges for pastors and church staff. We expect everyone to love what they do like we love what we do. It's the work of the Lord for crying out loud. From a sales standpoint, I understand the concept of shooting for the moon. At the same time, it is prudent for all of us to acknowledge the lives, schedules, and multiple demands on our volunteers' time. You will shoot yourself in the foot if your internal expectations are as high as your externally verbalized ones. So be smart and maintain proper expectations.

6. *Celebrate volunteers.* Everybody loves a pat on the back. You say, "But I'm not much of a backslapper." Well, I say, change your ways if you want to keep volunteers. Look for the good

in all that is done. Like paid staff members, volunteers need to be acknowledged when they perform to the expectations set. The more of this that happens, the greater the desire of the volunteer to "keep on trucking" and doing so with enthusiasm.

7. *Correct privately.* Wake up and smell the roses. There will certainly be times when something goes wrong. Volunteers are people with a huge capacity for failure. What you do with that failure will speak volumes as to how far a volunteer will grow in ministry. The more they grow, the farther the ministry will advance. When a mistake happens with a volunteer, never publicly point it out unless by mutual agreement with the volunteer and only for the teaching of a volunteer team. Pastors who quietly do this right grow ministries far beyond the level of ministries led by those who publicly destroy good people for their mistakes.

8. *Celebrate publicly.* When someone you asked to join you in ministry does something exceptional, make sure you shout it from the housetops. Really. Don't fall prey to "Well, we expected them to do that, and they did, so there's no need to celebrate." You'll lose with that one. You certainly cannot and should not celebrate every time an *i* is dotted or a *t* crossed, but you can celebrate publicly the exceptional ministry done by your highly valued volunteers. There will be

many volunteers who will pooh-pooh this, but you need to override them and publicly celebrate good things in ministry.

When done correctly, retaining volunteers creates stability in ministry worthy of the ministry itself. It is hard work. It is of high value. While it may not be glamorous, it will deliver the highest level of commitment and performance by the volunteers at the church you serve. Want to grow ministry? Retain volunteers.

SECTION 3
GUEST RETENTION

CHAPTER 12
THOUGHTS ON HOW TO RETAIN GUESTS WHO VISIT YOUR CHURCH PART 1

While the church Ric served was in the winter wonderland of North Dakota, he had no interest in the guests who visited his church feeling left out in the cold. He'd been to more conferences than you could shake a stick at. There were more systems out there that assured him he could easily close the back door by simply doing this, that and the other. He did this, and then he did that, and then he did the other—and guess what? The door was still open.

As Ric and I discussed Morningside Community Church's dilemma, I began to see a flaw in his thinking. As with any discussions with a client pastor when this happens, it is way better for the pastor to discover this than for me to just blurt out his shortcoming. Although some clients just want me to say it and solve it for them, in Ric's case, I knew he would need to own whatever process he embraced.

Along the way, I suggested to him it really did not make any difference what process from which conference he used. It was the unwritten pieces of retaining guests that seemed to escape him.

Front door, back door—we've all heard it and experienced it. We brag about how well we open the front door of our church to every person—rich, poor, black, white, educated or not. Then, like Ric, we cower when we think of the semi-truck–size double doors at the back of the church. Why does it have to be this way?

Let me provide a few thoughts on how your church might grow with the retention of the guests who visit week in and week out.

1. *Pray.* You can do all the planned steps in the world and skip this one, and you will find yourself not even at first base after a year of working hard at it. You must pray God will have his hand on all you do in reaching guests. Keep in mind he loves them way more than you want them to be part of the church. Pray for supernatural guidance in communicating his message to them. Pray your volunteers and you are prepared to truly receive guests as part of the family even before they look like they belong. Pray first and watch what happens with the rest.

2. *Prepare an experience.* What do they experience? When the guest walks through the doors of your church, how do they feel? What do their senses tell them about your church? What do they see and smell? Does the experience have a nice touch to it? The great thing for the church is that today's culture is highly experiential. This works to the advantage of a missional organization like the church that has at its core directing people to the experience of salvation. Because of this high value, it is imperative the church does all it can to create the greatest experience possible for the guests who attend.

3. *Consider the guest.* Think about what it must feel like to walk into your cozy, little church or your mammoth megachurch. The guest is just a regular Joe or Mary, single or couple, with or without kids. They've heard about the church and thought they'd try it out. What happens to them when they arrive? Do they know

- where to park?
- what door to enter?
- where the kiddos go?
- about the sanctuary/auditorium?
- where to sit?
- when to sit or stand?
- why to sit or stand?
- if they have to say anything?
- why there is group singing?
- if they have to give money, and if so, when do they do so, how much should they give?

4. *Consider your facilities.* This is one where too many throw up their hands in despair and say, "We can't afford it!" Hang on a minute. I'm not suggesting you break the bank or spend much of anything. I am suggesting you give the place a once-over, maybe twice-over if it's really bad. The problem with too many churches is they get way too comfortable with the old couch (figuratively) in the lobby. The family just kicks off their shoes (again, figuratively) at the front door, and nobody in the family thinks a thing of it. Your place needs to be impeccable in its appearance, inside and out. Neat as a pin.

Spotless. Shiny. Clean. Squeaky clean. Really neat. You can do this. If you are not the neat-freak type, then assign it with authority over to someone who is. Then, when one of the saints begins to observe this is not the comfortable, old church they remember, you'll know you are on your way. Until then, work, work, and work some more to make your facilities the best they can possibly be for the guests who visit.

There you have it, some worthy considerations for making your church the place for all guests. When you do these things, you will watch a great influx of guests begin to make the church the spiritual home for themselves and their families.

CHAPTER 13

THOUGHTS ON HOW TO RETAIN GUESTS WHO VISIT YOUR CHURCH PART 2

Pastor Lou had moved to Michigan from South Texas. He had a bit of a different twist on the retention dilemma. He and the church finally began to possess a culture of prayer. He understood the mind-set of the guest, worked hard to have the best of facilities, and really did provide a great experience each week for the guest. However, when it came to understanding how to connect church culture with community culture, that was a disaster. Muskegon was not McAllen. Further, the thoughts of training the volunteers to understand the guests seemed to be a time-consuming, unnecessary task. He thought he understood it for himself but even then was woefully short in that understanding.

When you think about the guests who will walk through the doors of your church over the next few weeks, what do you see? Further, how relevant to them is what you do? We know people have needs, and they know they are looking for answers. We know God and the Bible have those answers and that we are charged with the responsibility to communicate the same. But how can we keep them around long enough to see it happen?

Lots of stuff has been written on this subject, and your few minutes digesting this chapter is not going to quickly turn the mighty *Titanic* called *Your Church*.

But valuable spiritual discernment can be yours for consideration of the following as it relates to guests. The mission of the church is too important to not give thought to how we can do this thing called "guest retention" better.

1. *Acknowledge the Church culture.* This is a tough one for lots of churches. We've been conditioned to believe if we make many changes in how we look or what we do, we are selling our heritage down the river. Nothing could be farther from the truth. Once we as church leaders understand the necessity of addressing our church culture as it is seen by the guest, then we have a wonderful challenge before us: helping members—many of them long term—consider a church culture change. The reality is many church cultures are oil and water to many non-believer church guests. That is in large part why the church is not growing numerically. Our church culture is good for us because we get it. The guests don't. And if they don't, we need to address how we appear to them.

2. *Consider the community culture.* If you are a medium-sized community in the Northeast, you have a feel to your culture that is far different from Tupelo or San Francisco. You need to be a student of your culture and build the church to fit it. I can hear the screaming now from those who claim I'm suggesting we conform to the world. I am not. I *am* suggesting we be

wise as serpents and create something inside the church so the guest does not experience culture shock compared to their last stop at the local convenience store. It would kind of look like this. If your community is on the beach and everyone everywhere is wearing flowered shorts and shirts and flip-flops, you might not want to wear a three-piece suit. It doesn't fit the culture.

3. *Train volunteers.* You can read this chapter and draft a great plan, but if you do not communicate to the frontline volunteers who will have the greatest impact on whether a guest returns, it will all be for naught. The challenge with this is in communicating church culture versus community culture. Unfortunately, over the past number of decades, we have trained ourselves to believe church is about us. In particular, Sunday morning. This is where we reconnect with our friends, talk about the ball game or the latest with the kids. It is highly social. Not bad, just not focused on the main thing. You must train your volunteers when it comes to Sunday, it is all about the guest. Most churches would benefit greatly from following the advice of Mike Clarensau on the *audio podcast on guest retention* and considering the hospitality training offered by The Hardy Group at www.thehardygroup.org.

4. *Train yourself.* To state the obvious, you are your greatest asset and greatest liability. Most church leaders have much church-culture baggage

ingrained in themselves. Most of this needs to be unpacked and repackaged in a way that is guest friendly. Do not expect the guest to fit neatly into your preconceived idea of what they should look like or your clear recollection of what they did look like back in 2001. Train yourself to be relevant to the culture. If you are over forty, then draw and keep trusted people who are *under* forty near you. They may be your own kids or trusted young adults who know God and have been part of the church for a while. Train yourself to listen and change. If that is a challenge, then by all means pray for God's grace to do so. The guests are worth it!

While you look to the future in retaining guests, you should never lose sight of the fact God loves those guests more than you or I can imagine. We don't have to have a magic wand. We do have to be diligent in presenting all we are about in a way that culturally relates to them and ministers to their point of need, the greatest of which is their need of a savior. I pray to that end for you and your church.

CHAPTER 14

WHY DON'T GUESTS COME BACK TO OUR CHURCH?

With the flattened attendance Pastor Caleb was experiencing, he had become adept at asking the question, "Why don't guests come back to our church?" He always hoped there would be some quick and easy answer. There never was. So for four years, he looked at the stats and continued to do what he had always done. He forgot that the adage "Doing what you always have done and expecting different results is the definition of *insanity*." Caleb wasn't that far gone, but he clearly was not seeing a new future, and certainly the guests who visited the church weren't seeing any future. So maybe you're like Caleb, and you wonder why guests don't come back to your church either. Ever ask it?

Good question! I am glad you asked.

I have been in the business of church for thirty years, and this subject has no simple answers. However, there are some principles I would like to make note that might be helpful in your consideration of this issue for your church.

Are you doing things well? Of course, all of us say, "Yes, we are a church of excellence." That question, by the way, is tantamount to someone asking a person if they keep their kitchen clean. Almost everyone says yes to that one as well. But the reality is "clean" for one person is "not clean" for another. The same is true in churches.

I have been to plenty of churches where there is no other way to describe it other than just plain sloppy. It has a "home" feel for the home folks, but for the guests, it is a mess. So let's start here.

1. *Be better than Disney!* The hospitality must be superb. You say, "But we live in the North or Northeast, and our people are not as warm as those folks from the South." That is a lousy excuse. Get friendly and do it from the minute the guest enters your parking lot. Why not? Examine your hospitality and be willing to ratchet up your efforts with change. This is where everyone has the capacity to be better than everyone else—better than Disney, better than anyone! Be the best in hospitality.

2. *The restrooms and nurseries should be spic and span. No exceptions!* Need I say more?

3. *Visitation.* One of the things you must do is visit those who visit you. You might say, "We don't do that in our area of the country because it is culturally unacceptable to do so." Nice excuse but you asked the question above or at least picked up this book for some advice. On Monday, immediately following Sunday services, mobilize your troops, including the lead pastor, and get out and say thanks for coming to your church. That is the least you can do. Take your guests a small gift from the church while you are at it. You are not forcing your way into people's home. You are simply knocking on the

door, giving a gift, and saying thanks. If they invite you in, that is fine. Who knows, in that case, you might even be privileged to lead them across the line of faith to Jesus.

4. *Develop a turn-key guest system.* You must have a complete process to take people from their thought of attending your church all the way through to them coming onto the parking lot and entering your building. Then everything from deciding to come once, twice, three times, etc., to making a profession of faith, moving into discipleship and community, experiencing the joy of giving, and moving into full membership must be on your radar screen.

In addition to these core areas of church appearance and hospitality, be sure the three fundamental "sales" components of the church are in place: preaching, ministry in music, and ministry to children.

1. *The preaching needs to be good.* People want to hear Bible messages that are relevant to their lives. It does not have to be Billy Graham, but it has to be well prepared, well thought out, and well delivered. It might even be nice if it was anointed of God.

2. *The ministry in music has to be good.* It does not have to be Hillsong United, but it has to be good. Whether you like it or not, you are competing with some great music on the market today. So be good, well prepared, and fully directed by the

Spirit. If your church is still stuck in worship wars, you need to determine a way to whip that one. The new guest to your church who does not know God does not care what style of music is up for this week. It just has to be good music.

3. *The ministry to children has to be good.* The age group of adults with young children is one of the most fluid in ministry today. If you can minister in a meaningful way to a child age two or ten, you will capture the hearts of parents. Once a family buys into your children's ministry, you create an automatic feeder for your youth ministry in the years to come.

To answer your question as you think it before you ask it, "No, you don't have to wait until you have full-time staff to do these things." The issue is good preaching, good music, and good ministry to children. You can handle the good preaching, and good, qualified lay persons can do the other with your leadership.

So these are just a few starter-kit thoughts. Use these to zero in on the fundamentals.

1. Make the place as neat as a pin.

2. Do hospitality better than anyone else.

3. Preach good, relevant biblical messages.

4. Present good, current Christian worship music.

5. Have a children's ministry second to none.

If you do these things, guests will come once and come again. Do them, and you will be glad you did!

SECTION 4
PERSONAL LIFE

CHAPTER 15
PASTOR'S PERSONAL CHARACTER

Abraham Lincoln and Adolph Hitler both lived for fifty-six years. Michael W. Smith and Osama bin Laden were both born in 1957. When we think of Lincoln and Smith, we think of a set of character traits quite at odds with those exhibited by Hitler and bin Laden.

Character is that stuff way down, deep inside you. This is the stuff we talk about for which we are held accountable. It is the deepest, deepest character issues we struggle with or fully develop according to God's plan.

Luke 6:45 says, "The good person out of the good treasure of his heart produces good, and the evil person out of his evil treasure produces evil, for out of the abundance of the heart his mouth speaks." (ESV)

What happened on a bridge in Minneapolis in 2007? The I-35W Mississippi River Bridge was an eight-lane, steel truss arch bridge that carried Interstate 35W across the Mississippi River. During the rush hour on August 1, 2007, it suddenly collapsed, killing 13 people and injuring 145. Something at the bridge's core was flawed.

So what? I reference these four famous people and the 2007 bridge incident because they all communicate the building blocks of anything in life. Think candidly about the character building blocks of your life as a pastor. Your future is bright, but it is so only as you put the right character building blocks in place.

We operate with a basic sense of understanding of good character. However, we are born with a sinful nature, and if left to our own devices, we will not develop character that is good and pleasing to the Lord. We will constantly lean to our base nature.

How do you develop each of these ten traits in your own character?

1. *Honesty—free from deceit or fraud.* This can be one of the most difficult inner character traits to develop. From birth, we have developed an ability to lie to ourselves within. It is difficult to decipher whether we are true to ourselves or not. Here is how you can develop greater honesty within.

   - Always make sure what you think, feel, say, and do match up.
   - Always examine your motivation. Change the circumstances slightly to see if your actions would change.
   - It is an old line, but it is worth asking, "What would Jesus do?"

2. *Integrity—true and upright.* If you are a man or woman of high integrity, then people around you know what they see is what they get. Here are some considerations for building integrity into your life.

   - Be true in word and in action.
   - Always look for weaknesses within you and ask God to strengthen those areas or remove them if necessary.

- Be who people believe you to be, based on what you have said about you. Be sure what you tell them is true. Note: Do not be who people want you to be. There is a difference.

3. *Purity—free from inappropriate elements.* We often think of this in terms of sexual purity. This is a good focus for all ages and certainly for yours. To be pure you should do the following.
   - Think on those things that are pure and holy.
   - Avoid the appearance of evil while making sure the inner person matches the outer person.
   - Stay in the Word in order to live a life consistent with Scripture's guidance.

4. *Courage—the quality of the mind or spirit that enables a person to face difficulty, danger, pain, etc.* This trait does not mean you have to be the tough guy or girl. It does mean you stand for those things you consider right. Brian Tracy, a noted motivational speaker and author, suggests you do three things, and then I add a fourth.
   - Control your fear. This is easier said than done. Take every thought and fear captive.
   - Confront your fear. Look fear in the face and tell it what you will and will not accept.
   - Do your fear. When you allow God to use you to do something that previously petrified you, you will win over it.

- Look at other worthy leaders that seem to demonstrate courage and emulate their actions. Then make sure your actions match what is really inside you. Send courage inside if you need to.

5. *Confidence—belief in oneself and one's powers or abilities.* We are confident as the Lord gives us confidence. The problem is we look at others who look confident, and then we look deep within us. We lack confidence. We know we are really not as good as others think we are. We have successfully built a picture of ourselves that is not true. Note item 2 above.
    - Acknowledge God as your Creator.
    - Recognize God is your enabler.
    - Allow God to strengthen you.
    - Take a small step in accomplishing what God enables you to do.

6. *Humility—not proud or arrogant.* In a world of egos, this is tough. In the church world, we would rather our peers not ask us about how our church is doing if it is flat or declining. However, if it is on the increase, we are happy to take credit. Understand you can make good leadership decisions, but in the end, all of your decisions are from God. Be thankful and be humble.
    - Recognize all of your abilities are given by God and not by yourself.

- Develop your giftings and give all glory to God because they are his.
- Do not display phony humility.
- When people say good things about you, be gracious and defer all glory to God.
- Do not believe your press clippings.

7. *Kindness—of a good or benevolent nature or disposition.* This is a trait we too often interpret as being soft. As the leader of the church you serve, nothing about this is designed for you to be soft or weak. True kindness expressed to another can be one of your greatest strengths.
   - Ask God to sensitize you to the challenges others face.
   - While leading your leaders, look for opportunities to show genuine, nonmanipulative kindness to them.
   - Pray for a spirit that exudes kindness.

8. *Compassionate—possessing sympathy and tenderness toward others.* Our model at demonstrating compassion is Jesus. He could feel what people felt. While we as pastors try to advance the kingdom, we must never lose focus of the compassion necessary to be a leader like Jesus.
   - Ask God to help you see the needs of others and do something about them.
   - Seek to express compassion as Jesus did.
   - While leading with strength, touch with those who hurt.

9. *Loyalty—faithful to one's oath, commitments, or obligations.* This is probably the foundational trait asked for by lead pastors when hiring staff. At the same time, the lead pastor who understands and demonstrates loyalty to those around him is the one who merits the expression in return.

   • Ask God to create in you a commitment to people and for causes that align with his purposes for your life.
   • Be careful to always examine the mission of people and causes to which you are loyal.
   • Never fall prey to blind loyalty. Right is still right all the time.
   • Remember loyalty is a two-way street. Demonstrate it and also expect it from your team.

10. *Responsibility—answerable or accountable for something within one's power, control, or management.* The sooner each generation gets this one, the better. The sooner the young pastor gets this one, the better. Take it and be it. The leader who does is able to lead at higher levels than those who do not.

    • Never play the blame game.
    • If you are anywhere near at fault, take responsibility.
    • Encourage others to demonstrate this trait while modeling it for them.

At the end of the day, you have to ask yourself, "Am I who God wants me to be?" Often we ask, "Am I doing what God wants me to do?" Although "doing" is good, "being" is best. Once you "are," then you will "do."

As you consider your future in ministry, it is the development of your personal character that will dictate how far you can go in God's eyes. Do all you can to be honest and maintain integrity in all your dealings. Be responsible and be pure. Be courageous, loyal, and confident. Be humble, kind, and compassionate. When you are, you win, and more importantly, the kingdom wins.

You are on a great journey. As God enables you, I encourage you to be of impeccable character, and God will be pleased.

CHAPTER 16

WHY SHOULD A PASTOR HAVE A LARGE NETWORK OF FRIENDS?

Friends make the world go round. That's the way Jerry had viewed things back in his administrator days. But the daily grind of lead pastoring had taken its toll on his relationships with those who had been close to him. Back in the day when he and Caitlin were having kids and their friends were doing the same, it was like one big networking feast—friends having them over and meeting other new friends and the Morans returning the favor.

Over time Jerry had become so focused on improving the church he lost sight of doing those things that would improve him. One of those was the continual development of his network of friends, both personally and professionally. By the time Jerry and I connected, he was down to one other pastor friend in another state with whom he connected from time to time—and me! Jerry was at the point where when he had questions, there were few places to turn to find answers. He had failed to cultivate his network of friends.

So why is it a pastor should have a large network of friends? Answer: Because pastors are supposed to influence as many people on earth for Jesus as possible. Simple.

However, it's not so simple for lots of men and women who stand in our pulpits week in and week out.

Sometimes pastors have, over the time of their ministry, come to view "networking" as secular and clearly not something a pastor should do. It smacks of wrongly motivated maneuvering for something that should only be done by God.

Let me suggest a different way of thinking about networking. Networking is a very good thing. It is the thing where partnerships and collaboration are made. Networking in the kingdom of God is about meeting more people, advancing more biblical causes, and rightly being positioned to respond to God's call in your life.

While working in the college environment for almost five years, I enjoyed listening to twenty-year-olds pontificate on the high ideals of never kissing up to anyone, of only letting God direct them to the right person at the right time. That was their way of saying, "I am afraid to talk to people I do not know, so I will meet no one and let God do it."

I loved these students. I also loved to engage their brains on what God could do if they, the student, would act in a way that was proactive and did not just sit on the sideline. How wise it is for a student to meet guest chapel speakers and guest classroom instructors. How wise it is to look for ways to branch out beyond the typical college crowd.

To meet the president of the college or university and to make sure he or she knows your name is of inestimable value. I cannot tell you the number of times when as an administrative pastor of two different megachurches, I called a college president and said to him, "Can you give me the names of your top 1 or 2 students who have exceptional leadership and pastoral capacity?" The names that came to that president's minds were names he knew. So the idealist student who considered all networking as kissing-up lost.

I had contact made with me by two pastor-friends a number of months ago, both expressing an interest in moving from their current lead pastorate to another. Both were good guys. One had a network, and he pastored a church of 470. The other did not, and he pastored a church of 800.

Guess which pastor became the new lead pastor of a church on the East Coast of two thousand people poised for phenomenal growth. Answer: the guy with the network. The pastor without the network was unknown. Good people who were advising the church did not know him and hence did not know of the good ministry he was a part of. They did not know others who knew him because there were so few others. It was sad for that pastor, but true.

Let's take a look at why a pastor without a network is limited in his influence for the kingdom.

1. Their world is small.

2. Their ability to make new things happen is limited.

3. The word of the good things God does in their ministry is restricted to their small corner of the world.

4. Their ability to appropriately advance in their own ministry is limited.

This last point can rankle our spiritual sensitivities. Somehow we have come to believe to be isolated from a network is best, and that proves only God is making things happen. We have the wrong thinking that to appropriately advance in our own ministry is wrong. Here is the problem with that line of thinking. God does his work on earth through us. He always has and always will. So why should not the "us" part of that equation be bigger and bigger and bigger? Why should your ministry remain smaller when it could be bigger?

Further, why would any pastor want *any* of the four things listed above to be part of their life or ministry? That makes no sense. Any lead pastor with any drive to do anything for God needs the biggest world possible with minimal limitations. The church world needs to know what is working in that pastor's ministry, and they need to be positioned to reach more people with the gospel. Yes, reaching more people is better than reaching fewer people. Numbers are everything.

Networks are good. Networks get more things done, better and quicker. Why in the world would you as a lead pastor, the one responsible to lead your body of believers to the highest spiritual heights possible, not want to connect with more people?

Here is what a network should do for any pastor serious about reaching lost people. That is what we are about, isn't it?

1. It allows a pastor to know who is doing what.

2. It gives credence to methods in ministry that work.

3. It allows a pastor to be mentored by association. Whether young or old, rubbing shoulders with other good pastors is valuable. You would be amazed what you can pick up by association.

4. Not networking makes you stale.

5. Good athletes learn from great athletes. If you want to be a great pastor in God's eyes, if you want to share the gospel with more people than you have ever shared with before, go hang around people who do that. Network.

6. When something needs to be done, your network can help you get it done.

7. Your network gives you a broader view of the body of Christ. Why would you want to know fewer fellow believers?

Further, we are wrong to believe somehow all networking is wrongly motivated. I do not question to build a network motivated by ego, money, or fame is to build in vain from God's perspective. However, to build a network to do more for the kingdom, to reach more lost people, to share the gospel with thousands rather than hundreds is all a very good thing.

There you have it. Build your network. Whether you're twenty, forty, sixty, or eighty, it is time to get started. There is no time like the present to know more people, to reach more people, and to advance the mission of the church through your network.

Now is the time, and you are the one. Go after it!

CHAPTER 17

I'M NOT GOOD ENOUGH OR SMART ENOUGH

For all Pastor Lou's great strengths in helping Northgate Church be a leading church in Michigan, he dealt with a deep, personal insecurity not uncommon to many pastors. He flat out did not feel good enough or smart enough to lead the church to the level he wanted and knew God had for them. Although not the valedictorian in his Bible college graduating class, he certainly wasn't a C- student either.

I remember a day when he was telling me how awkward he felt in challenging the church to believe in all God could do through them while he was personally having all sorts of doubts about what God could do through him.

Ever felt like Lou? Good! That's just where God wanted Lou and where he wants you. Trite statement, you say? Not so!

Think about it. Suppose you are God, and you look around on earth to find someone to lead the church in your community. If you think long and hard on the issue, you certainly would not put you in charge. You are not good enough, smart enough, or even spiritual enough to lead this church.

God knows that and a whole lot more about you and every other pastor who could be a prospect to lead this church. If the truth be told, it would scare the livin' daylights out of all of us if we knew about our leaders' inadequacies.

This is a given. No one knows it all. So how do you internally handle the lack of knowledge? After all the cute, little spiritual (and true) statements are made, you are still you. You still know your own limitations, and the "livin' daylights" are being scared out of you as you think about leading into the future.

Let's focus.

1. *You are called.* It is a given you have been called by God to serve in your local church. It has grown bigger than you envisioned; nonetheless, you are the pastor.

2. *The alternative.* The alternative of you feeling very adequate to the task at hand would be alarming to say the least. The adequate-feeling pastor either pastors a very stagnant church or they are on the path to self-confidence and self-destruction.

3. *Join the club.* You can be assured virtually every pastor, in a church of any size at all, feels very inadequate to do the job God has asked of them. Welcome to the club!

4. *Your sufficiency is in the Lord.* That is not a trite statement. It is true, and if you don't remember it, you are in big trouble!

5. *Maintain your dependence on God.* You need God like you have never needed him before. It is

for that reason he will get all the glory as the increase continues to come.

6. *Who wrote that?* While you acknowledge your inadequacy, also acknowledge your dependence on God. He will provide for your ability to do any task he assigns you. I've seen it written someplace that with God, all things are possible! Hmmmm...where was that?

With those elements noted, I encourage you to relax and rest in God's call on your life. Know he has not given you any task without the divine backup to do that task at hand.

Revel in the seeming foolishness of a supreme being—our god—calling a very much un-supreme person—you—to reach his people. The fact his—not *your*—church is growing is the ultimate sign you are not in charge. He is!

If I were you, after I get over the enormity of that statement, I would marvel at how little, old you could be so fortunate to be inadequate, privileged, and called by such a big God. This happens so you can share his gospel with a lost and dying world in your community.

You, my friend, are the most blessed pastor in America. In over your head? Rest in that!

CHAPTER 18

I'M WORN OUT: WHAT DO I DO?

In Lou's case, if feeling inadequate wasn't enough, the guy was wearing out to boot. He'd been at the church for almost seventeen years; the kids were either off to college or finishing up high school. Life should be good. While he did not classify himself as a workaholic, he was quick to admit he would burn the candle at too many ends. With family and close friends, the word *lazy* was 180 degrees from Lou.

The years had taken their toll. Now a great servant of the Lord was staring blankly at his computer, at me, at his wife, at the church—at everything. What was he to do?

Wow! It's a good thing Lou had chosen a "cushy" profession for his life's work. Probably the same for you. Just think what it would have been like if you had chosen a tough job where you were on call 24/7, had to be "up" all the time, and had to deal with one or two cantankerous people. That would really be tough!

You obviously know the previous paragraph is the ultimate tongue-in-cheek. You have a very challenging and rewarding job as a pastor. The expectations on you are high. Depending on your situation, the demands may be excessive, and for whatever reason, you are just shot. Worn out, drained, caput—there's nothing left! If that is the case, please know there is hope.

The time it has taken you to get into this position has obviously taken its toll on you. I bet this did not happen overnight. It probably built for some number of weeks, maybe months, or even years.

I remember one time I looked at my church and family schedule and realized I was out in the evening in some way or another for sixty-three days straight. I know the critic of my sixty-three-day marathon schedule would say not all of it was work related so don't blame the ministry for it. I wasn't. But I was absolutely exhausted! I had multiple components of my life: church, family, personal. And when all totaled, they took their toll on me.

You probably can relate to what happened to me. Maybe now it is you. So what do you do about it?

Realize reading this chapter and developing a plan of action will not result in rest within twenty-four hours. It probably will be many days or weeks before you begin to find rest. Sorry I could not be more optimistic for you. That is the real world.

Based on my experience, here is what I suggest you do. Remember, this is a long-term solution. Fixing your lack-of-rest issue will not happen overnight.

1. *Think and pray.* Find a time to stop what you are doing, even though your tasks are very good and necessary. Do these two things in earnest: think and pray. If you say, "I can't stop anything," then I say, "Stay tired."

2. *Primary groups.* Define for yourself the primary groups to which you have responsibilities. The

Right Turns |

groups might be something like family, personal, and church.

3. *Highest priority.* Write down those highest-priority items (listed in order) you must do in order to fulfill your obligations to each of those groups. Maybe list three to five items for each group.

4. *What are the consequences?* Note to yourself what would be the consequences of saying no to one or two of the lower priority items for each group. I know they are called priority items, but if you are worn out, you need to say no even to very good items. This will help you identify some things to which you should say no.

5. *Family issues?* There may not be a lot of family items you eliminate.

6. *Personal issues?* There may be some personal issues you can eliminate. However, make sure you do not eliminate those things that contribute to your spiritual and physical well-being.

7. *Mission driven?* When evaluating your tasks at the church, ask yourself these things: What is the mission of the church? Does what I do advance the mission of the church? Be extremely critical of the answer to this one. We tend to lump everything we do for the church in the category of working toward the mission of the church when in reality many tasks do not advance the church's mission.

117 |

8. *What if I say no?* You should ask yourself, "What happens if I say no to this task?" Don't answer this with, "My whole city will go to hell if I don't do this." It won't!

You have to start saying no. I know you're thinking, "Easy for you to say." I know it is tough to do, but if you sincerely seek help, your only answer is to begin saying no. If you are in a church where saying no is not tolerated, then maybe your days there are numbered. I do know if you are worn out, the way to find rest is to begin to take things off your plate, and that only happens when you say no to some things.

If you don't want to follow this advice, then good luck. Stay tired. Don't rest. Be worn out and pay the price. However, by following advice I've listed, I believe you will identify some light at the end of the tunnel.

Start today, and maybe two, four, six, or eight weeks from now, you will write me and say, "Wow! It was tough, but I said no to some very good things. The church did not fall apart. The mission is still intact, and I have my life back." Let's pray to that end!

CHAPTER 19

SEVEN OBSERVATIONS FOR SABBATICAL REST

It didn't take a rocket scientist to identify a major reason for Lou's dilemma. He *was* worn out. He was not able to keep the pace he had charted for seventeen years, and now he was paying a price for it. He did not succumb to any moral or ethical failure, but he was empty. Ever felt that way? In his case, Lou needed rest, a lot of it.

Rest. Oh, to get more of it.

I had a pastor recently say to me he made a challenge statement to his youth pastor. The youth pastor was looking for a break. "You have no idea what real work is. If you were in the real world, the business culture, you would see what real work is." If the youth pastor was truly lazy, then the pastor made the correct assessment.

Unfortunately, if the youth pastor was not, then I'm concerned this lead pastor had been in ministry so long he had lost sight of the fact the work in the local church is some of the most intense on the planet. In most cases, the work of the ministry is truly hard work, and the need for a break is critical to the long-term health of the church and the pastor.

Let me note: this does not imply we work harder or longer than the laity. Lots of people in the church work long, hard hours. However, the spiritual component of what pastors do brings a dimension of pressure and stress to their lives' work that is unique to the ministry.

We can get caught up in idealizing the aura of business and industry in this area. In many cases, there is much value in doing so. However, we should never minimize the intensity of what we do. In that vein, there is a time for extended rest.

I would like to give you some thoughts on sabbatical rest. A sabbatical is a rest from work or a hiatus. I will not break new ground in what you are reading regarding sabbaticals. However, I challenge you to take care of yourself and those who work with and for you. Work hard and then *rest well*.

Here are some quick observations I make on the value of taking a sustained period of time off called a sabbatical.

1. *Spiritual renewal.* This is the single component that differentiates a pastor's sabbatical from virtually every other career field. Because pastors eat, sleep, and breathe in the spiritual world, there comes a point where they need to come apart from the work of the ministry before they truly come apart. This time away is perfect for God to speak to the quieted spirit within us.

2. *Physical winding down.* It will take you at least seven days and maybe more to bring your body to a slowed pace to actually relax. Physical rest will truly begin to set in when this happen.

3. *Emotional winding down.* It will take an equally long period of time for your emotions to begin to settle down. Those stresses and emotional drains will begin to ebb from your life, and a

true sense of relaxation will set in. You will be amazed at just how relaxed you can be when your emotions are not all over the map.

4. *Relationships improve.* Presuming you take your sabbatical with your spouse, you will find your time together to be enriched. The pace of running your life by the clock will defer to the ease of spending time, extended time together. The stronger the pastor's marital relationship, the more secure the body feels as it moves forward.

5. *Vision clears.* Your ability to separate wild and crazy ideas from true vision for the future will become clear. There may be times on your sabbatical you set aside to think about your own personal future. Depending on the designs of your sabbatical, it may be that vision for your ministry can become part of the mix. The ability to focus is increased.

6. *Planning increases.* If planning for the future is part of your sabbatical, the ability to do so without the clutter of phone, e-mail, correspondence, and emergencies is increased dramatically. Consequently, the resulting plan is of greater value to the church and its leadership.

7. *Church benefits.* The church learns the staff and volunteers who serve so capably when you are physically at the helm are more than capable in carrying the day in your absence. Further, a renewed pastor results in a renewed congregation.

The body responds positively to the refreshing in their pastor. It can be said sabbaticals, when implemented properly, can contribute to the numerical, financial, and spiritual growth of the church because the leader comes back firing on all cylinders as opposed to when they left firing on only half of them.

When embarking on the idea of a sabbatical, a number of things need to be put in place. The pastor and their key leadership team should answer the following questions (not an exhaustive list). These answers will drive the sabbatical and put in place its success.

1. When will the sabbatical take place?

2. Is the budget prepared to cover the cost of the sabbatical and the cost of replacement pulpit-fill and related expenses?

3. How long will the sabbatical be?

4. How will the church cover the responsibilities of the one on sabbatical?

5. How do we ensure the pastor's desk will be cleared and e-mail and voice mail will be empty upon his or her return?

6. How will emergencies be handled?

7. Who has the authority to contact the pastor in case of an emergency, specifically related to them or their family? How are those emergencies defined?

8. How do we communicate to the church the benefit of a pastoral sabbatical?

The leadership must be wise in its establishment and implementation of a sabbatical policy. Go to www.thehardygroup.org to download a sample sabbatical policy. Communicating the significant benefit to the church is critical. Having a renewed pastor in the pulpit, delivering the word of God out of the refreshing in his spirit acquired on the sabbatical, will bring a renewal to the body as a whole.

I recommend a pastor's sabbatical be one to two months in length. Anything less is really just a vacation. Anything more leaves more at risk than necessary. The natives tend to get restless near the end of a time away of more than two months. It can be done, but I encourage caution. Further, I recommend a sabbatical every five to seven years. For multiple staff churches, it makes sense to rotate the sabbaticals so as to not increase the extended absences of more than one pastor at a time.

The time is now for you to begin your preparation for next year's sabbatical. To this end, if you need help from The Hardy Group, please do not hesitate to contact us through the website www.thehardygroup.org or e-mail me directly at dhardy@thehardygroup.org. In the meantime, work hard and plan to rest very, very well. A well-planned sabbatical takes you there. You and your board will not regret what it will do for you and what it will do for your church.

Rest is yours if you take it. The ministry God has called you to is more than worthy of your time away to be the best you can be upon your return. May God bless you on this journey.

SECTION 5
STAFFING

CHAPTER 20

THIRTEEN NONNEGOTIABLES BETWEEN LEAD AND STAFF PASTORS

I have a pastor friend in San Diego that has only pastored his current church and previously a great church in suburban Kansas City. Brian is a no-nonsense kind of guy who, by the way, is the only guy I know of who had three sons all seven years apart in age. He truly is on tap to have a son entering college, one entering middle school and one entering kindergarten. Wow!

He had compiled a great list of what we are calling nonnegotiables between lead and staff pastors. He admittedly probably ripped some of the concepts off a mentor pastor of his, Charlie Tuttle in McKinney, Texas. As with all things in ministry, we share what we've learned with everyone who will read or listen. Brian, Charlie and I would both admit this list is probably not comprehensive in nature, but it sure is a good start on how pastoral staff members should relate to their leader.

Most lead pastors have collegial relationships with their staff guys and gals in ministry. These same pastors relationally flow with the ups and downs in ministry, and their teams keep moving forward. All sorts of interactions have flexibility, and circumstances dictate responses. However, for lead pastors of larger, growing churches, there are certain nonnegotiables in how staff pastors interact with and on behalf of the lead pastor.

This may not be an exhaustive list, but it is a starting point for consideration.

1. *Staff pastors cannot obligate lead pastors for anything, but staff pastors can represent lead pastors in all matters.* Because staff pastors are an extension of the lead pastor's office, staff pastors represent lead pastors in ministry; however, staff pastors do not always know the lead pastor's personal or professional schedule. Therefore without the lead pastor's permission, staff pastors cannot obligate lead pastors to anything, i.e., "Pastor will call you today."

2. *Always communicate up the ladder.* Lead pastors would rather have too much information than not enough.

3. *If staff pastors make a mistake, they should tell the lead pastor first.* Generally this will be the end of it. This allows the lead pastor to represent the staff pastor to the affected body and the board if necessary. It also creates unity and stability within the church when they feel everyone is on the same page, especially if a mistake has taken place.

4. *Let nothing fester inside you! Nothing!* Staff pastors must protect their hearts at all times. If a staff pastor is carrying an offense toward the lead pastor or someone else on the team, it will surface. It will be revealed at the wrong time and place. Deal with it immediately.

5. *Lead and staff pastors are a team—think win-win situations.* While staff pastors work for and with lead pastors, they must all think about how they can work to make the other win. The same exists for lead pastors. There is no such thing as win-lose. If there is a loss on either side of the ledger, everyone loses.

6. *Everybody can be a jerk except you.* Before a staff pastor's name is the sacred title of *pastor.* Because all pastors are held to a higher standard in life and ministry, pastors do not have the luxury of "losing it." Always take the higher ground. People in the church can be brutal, but pastors can never react in any situation in a negative manner.

7. *Present a united front at all times—especially when staff pastors disagree.* Learn how to represent the lead pastor's heart and other staff pastors' hearts even when in disagreement. Always speak positively this way. Again, this creates stability and unity.

8. *Do your best. Always!* Enough said.

9. *Never say we can't do something, or it's impossible.* Lead pastors of larger, growing churches simply do not think like this.

10. *Never abuse privileges.* Lead pastors often have open-door policies. Lead pastors often make themselves professionally and personally

available to staff pastors 24/7. Staff pastors should never abuse the privilege.

11. *Staff pastors are an extension of the lead pastor's office.* For example, because in larger churches lead pastors cannot do youth ministry and be the lead pastor at the same time, they hire a youth pastor. In this case, because a youth pastor is an extension of the lead pastor's office, the youth pastor should be carrying the vision, mission, and purpose of the organization to the students of the church. One church, one path, traveled together.

12. *If a staff pastor cannot support and follow the lead pastor's lead and vision, the staff pastor should resign.* If the resignation is initiated by the staff pastor, the lead pastor and the church can celebrate all the staff pastor has done and have a great send-off. A not-so-good alternative to a staff-pastor-initiated resignation under these circumstances could mean the lead pastor may have to ask the staff pastor to leave.

13. *Everything communicates something.* Absolutely everything! Therefore, staff pastors must watch and guard all words, responses, and actions.

When staff and lead pastors interact with these nonnegotiables in clear focus, the mission of the church moves forward. All staff members hit on all cylinders when this happens, and the lead pastor has multiplied effectiveness through their staff.

CHAPTER 21

TEN THOUGHTS FOR LEAD PASTORS IN LEADING THEIR MUSIC/WORSHIP PASTORS

Ric was fortunate. The existing music/worship pastor at his North Dakota church was extremely gifted and clicked immediately with Ric as soon as the Schultzes arrived in Fargo. He told me for all the horror stories he heard from his pastor friends in working with the artsy, musician types, he was building a great set of stories on how a lead pastor could work well together with his music/worship pastor.

Ric and I have both heard statements like, "This music pastor I have is the best on Sunday morning, but working with them during the week can be challenging." This is a stronger-than-normal response some pastors give me when describing the interpersonal workings between themselves and the music pastor who serves the church. Unfortunately, for some lead pastors and their music pastor, it is too close to true. Of all staff interactions, this one can be the most tricky to navigate.

To set the stage on any writing of this nature, I must clearly communicate the ground rules for engagement between the lead pastor and their music pastor. While there is give and take on both parts in any staff working relationship, it is important to remember the lead pastor leads. They set the stage for how the interactions occur. The music pastor, while gifted and a leader in their own right, must understand the order of leadership in the church. At the same time, healthy debate and challenge should exist in this relationship. When these roles are understood, the road is much smoother than it would be otherwise.

Here are some thoughts for your consideration in your role in leading the music pastor on your team.

1. *Pray for the music pastor.* This can be one of the most overlooked aspects of our working relationships with music pastors. Although we sometimes say blanket prayers for the whole team, it is critical individual staff members are lifted to the Lord. Pray the Spirit of the Lord be on the music pastor. Pray they are renewed in their mind as they seek after him. Pray their music will uplift Jesus's name and will draw the body into worship. Pray for an anointing on their ministry. Pray for your relationship with the music pastor. Pray, pray, and pray again.

2. *Lead with confidence.* There are not many things worse than for a leader not to lead. The lead pastor must constantly be in a position to lead and to do so with confidence. While interactions must occur between the lead pastor and the music pastor, the lead pastor must be confident in what they want to happen during a worship service. The lead pastor will generally agree to the flow the music pastor suggests. However, to be reticent to challenge the music pastor is disastrous. You must challenge when necessary. Do so with confidence. This does not mean you

have to be a dictator. It does mean you must lead with confidence.

3. *Earn the right to be followed.* It is important the music pastor has confidence in the lead pastor's leadership. In demonstrating the confidence just described, the lead pastor merits confidence from the music pastor. The lead pastor should always work to remain worthy of being followed by the music pastor in prayer, personal lifestyle, decision making, and the modeling of godly leadership. In most of life, we can be followed because people are required to follow us, or we can be followed because we have earned the right to be followed. Earn the right!

4. *Be secure.* Don't worry about the fact people say nice things about the music pastor's worship leading ability. For goodness' sake, you hired the guy or gal. You are who you are as designed by God, and so is the music pastor. Be secure. You don't have to be them, and you don't want them to be you. Rather than get insecure about yourself in relationship to the music pastor, celebrate their value to you and the body in worship. God picked you to lead the church and the music pastor to walk with you in that journey. Be secure.

5. *Listen.* There are few things worse than a leader who will not listen. In the working relationship with the music pastor, it is critical the lead pastor exercise great listening skills. You do

not have to agree with the music pastor on all counts, although if you have the right person in place, you generally will. However, if you ever get to a point where the music pastor thinks you are not listening or valuing their ideas or spiritual intuition, you short-circuit the most critical relationship of the Sunday experience of drawing people to God. Listen well.

6. *Take advantage of the music pastor's artistry.* Music pastors sometimes get a bad rap for having an attitude. Sometimes they deserve it. Some lead pastors see the music person as temperamental. Frankly, anybody can have a temperament issue, but music pastors and their artistic ways get hit with this one the most. Do not fight it. Don't try to make your music pastor think or operate like your church treasurer or administrator. They are wired differently, and on Sunday morning when they lead the congregation into the beauty of worship, you are glad for that. Allow the art and creative giftings of the music pastor to augment your pulpit. During the worship service, there needs to be a coordinated flow of everything. However, in the planning phases of the service, give the music pastor the freedom to be creative in how they contribute to the service. You and the church win when this happens.

7. *Challenge the music pastor.* No matter where your music pastor is on the talent and skill level, they always need to be challenged. I watch this role

get stuck because the music pastor reaches a level of excellence and then is never challenged to move farther. This is sad. Certainly the music pastor should challenge themselves. The lead pastor must always challenge the music pastor to be better and to reach higher. I have never seen a church that has arrived in praise and worship. There is always more for the body to experience. There is always more for a music pastor to bring to the table. While you never want to get the label of *unable to please*, you must always applaud where the music pastor has brought you and then challenge them to the new place where the church can go.

8. *Give recognition to the music pastor.* Seldom do pastors do things for the applause of men, or at least they should not, it is always advisable to apply the *thank-you* part of that which we learned as children—to say, "Please and thank you." Even the most confident music pastor benefits from appropriately placed accolades of a job well done. Doing so in sincerity gains the lead pastor relational capital when times get tough.

9. *Set clear expectations.* Setting clear expectations at the beginning of your relationship with the music pastor will save you all sorts of headaches later on. You should acknowledge the music pastor is the skilled pastor in this field of ministry. At the same time, as the leader,

you need to make sure they understand your expectations. Do not assume.

10. *Be flexible.* Whenever possible, give the music pastor the benefit of the doubt. Flex with them. Realize as much as you want them to hit it out of the park every week, they might miss one or two like you do in the pulpit. Be flexible.

When you do these things, the church you lead and its music pastor will see some of the greatest days ever. Why settle for the good of the past when the better and best of the future can be yours with music and praise and worship? God has given you a talent in your music pastor. Celebrate it and develop it within them. Together you can applaud what God does in your midst.

CHAPTER 22

TEN THOUGHTS FOR MUSIC/WORSHIP PASTORS IN SERVING THEIR LEAD PASTORS

The music/worship pastor working with Ric was a guy by the name Bill McKinley. He was a cool guy, thirty years old, married with two daughters. He could do the contemporary music in his sleep and was well versed in doing enough blended music to keep the older saints satisfied.

However, Bill's greatest contribution to the church was his understanding of his role in serving the lead pastor. Bill's ego had long ago gone in check, and he lived to make worship the launching pad to his lead pastor's sermons. When Ric arrived, they hit it off immediately, and Bill did all he could to communicate his desire to help Ric reach more and more spiritually lost people with the gospel. He would do so with his music and worship.

The farthest statement from Bill's lips was, "I wish he would let me do the music, and he do the preaching." I have heard this one from more music pastors than I care to remember. While there certainly can be cases where the lead pastor micromanages beyond his skill level, in the cases of the quote above, the music pastor did not understand their role in serving the lead pastor.

It is true lead pastors have opinions about music and how it is done. That is okay. By the way, they are the boss. One of the early things music pastors need to understand is the buck stops with the lead pastor. I know we are all about the team, but the buck stops with them. While we want to feel some independence to do what we know to be the best musically, the lead pastor is the one who takes the lion's share of the heat if things go wrong. Hence, lead pastors have opinions, and they exercise them.

In most cases, the relationship between the music pastor and the lead pastor can be the richest of all staff relationships. These two positions feed off each other and bring clarity to what the church service is all about.

Here are some thoughts for consideration in serving the lead pastor on the team and making the worship experience the best it can be for the congregation.

1. *Pray for the lead pastor*. If you do everything else but fail to do this one, you lose. It is critical to understand prayer is necessary for your relationship to work smoothly with the lead pastor. Pray for the lead pastor's family, prayer life, ministry, vision, health, and future. That's just for starters. Then realize the lead pastor needs to be renewed in their mind and spirit. Pray all they put their hands to will produce souls for the kingdom.

2. *Be a worshipper yourself*. You cannot take people where you have not been. Neither can you take the people to a destination where you are uncertain yourself. Never allow your role as the music pastor to supersede your role as a son or daughter of God. The lead pastor needs you to be

in direct communion with God. When you are, you are better for the lead pastor because there will be a greater sense of connectedness between the two of you in following the Lord and in leading the service. Always be a worshipper.

3. *Invest in yourself.* Never get to the point where you know it all and can no longer learn. When that happens, you have lost significant effective value for the lead pastor and for yourself for that matter. Always continue to grow. Look for ways that are inexpensive or free to bring greater value to your ministry. As you grow and develop, the lead pastor is able to hand more off to you. Talk with your lead pastor about the continuing educational opportunities available to music pastors. Budgets can be tight, but smart use of budgeted dollars can make you better.

4. *Reinvent yourself.* Music changes so quickly it is important for you to maintain the highest of value for your lead pastor. Some churches are not as quick to adopt change in music as others. However, at all times, the music pastor needs to continue to refine who they are as a musician, a person, and a child of God. Always continue to grow. This becomes particularly acute the longer the music pastor moves into their late forties and into their fifties. The lead pastor and the church cannot afford to have you fall into a rut of doing things the way they have always been done. Although some in the church would call for that, the masses of people who do not know

God clamor for more. Reinvent yourself early and often.

5. *Be flexible.* There are not many things worse for a lead pastor to deal with than a music pastor who is completely inflexible. In fact, that will send the music pastor out the door faster than most things. Besides, it stifles what God wants to do in the worship service. As hard as it is for some music pastors to understand, it is not about them. They are key players in bringing the worship service together, but they must both personally and professionally exhibit all the flexibility in the world. The lead pastor needs that in you, so give it to him. Be flexible and watch what God will do in and through you.

6. *Be humble.* While we all enjoy being recognized for what we do, this issue of humility stares all of us in the face. Most music pastors dismiss this too frequently. It is necessary in all interaction with the lead pastor that the music pastor maintains humility. While they may be extraordinarily gifted musically, they must never allow that gifting to get in the way of what God wants to do in advancing the church. The relationship with the lead pastor can be strained by pride on the part of the music pastor. Stay humble before God. Celebrate what God does in your ministry but always stay humble. Give all glory and honor to the Lord for that which is done in the body.

7. *Develop spiritual creativity.* It is critical even
   the seasoned music pastor continue to develop
   spiritual creativity within them. Never allow
   the routine of doing the worship teams, band
   rehearsals, choirs, ensembles, etc., to get in the
   way of what God may want to create inside you.
   Your best value to the lead pastor will be seen as
   you continue to create new and more effective
   ways of doing music and bringing the body into
   the presence of the Lord.

8. *Understand the lead pastor's role.* No one really
   knows what it is like to sit in the lead pastor's
   chair until you have sat there. You must know
   while you ask for those things that will advance
   the music ministry at the church, there are
   others who ask the lead pastor for a multitude of
   other things to advance their corner of ministry
   at the church. The lead pastor is responsible for
   it all. The smart staff member will be sensitive
   to that and in all their interactions with the lead
   pastor will defer to this reality. Lead pastors are
   grateful when staff members interact with them
   with this understanding.

9. *Run interference for the lead pastor.* This should
   be every staff member's job. Always watch out
   for the lead pastor. The music pastor, more than
   any other, should have the spiritual heart of the
   lead pastor. In this way, it is possible for the
   music pastor to see and hear things through the
   lead pastor's filter. When this happens the music

pastor can anticipate things for the lead pastor and help stave off conflicts that could arise. Many times, these conflicts can be avoided with the wise intervention of a skilled music pastor who runs interference for the lead pastor.

10. *Understand mission.* Central to all you do as the music pastor is the mission of the church. Those who lose sight of our responsibility to reach and teach those who do not know God often find themselves in a quagmire of debate over style and preferences far askew from the real issue at hand. It becomes all about music, and it clearly is not that. The mission of the church is the greatest on the planet. Music is key to people coming to an understanding of that mission. Music pastors who understand are able to advance the vision of the lead pastor in greater ways than otherwise possible.

At the end of the day, the tally sheet needs to show you as the music pastor did all you could to advance the ministry of the lead pastor. Did you lift their ministry to the point of advancing the kingdom in your community? If you did, then my hat is off to you. Continue to do the list above, and God will bring great increase to the church you and the lead pastor are privileged to serve.

CHAPTER 23

FIVE REASONS SECOND-CHAIR LEADERS LIFT FIRST-CHAIR LEADERS

While Caleb Chutter was continuing to come to grips with the necessity for the church to truly change if it wanted to improve, he was blessed to have a couple of team members that was helping him to that end. One of them was Reid Masterson. Pastor Reid served as Caleb's administrative pastor and was the definition of a servant. Reid learned early on how to lift Caleb in order to advance Caleb's efforts of change and improvement.

Reid's view was, "If I am in the second chair, I should know why I'm concerned about lifting the first-chair leader I serve?" In an age where it is "all about me" it only makes sense to take time to flesh out some reasons why second-chair leaders need to lift the first-chair leaders they serve. Most first-chair leaders are strong in their leadership, and ideally, they have placed themselves around nearly as strong second chairs.

When a second-chair leader is able to hit full stride, they are able to bring strengths to the church, and the lead pastor that could only have been dreamed of in days gone by. Advancing mission and the cause of the gospel needs to ride front and center for these servants of the church.

There are all sorts of how-to books in the church market today. Some address the how-to's of being a second-chair leader. However, very little is written as to *why* a second-chair leader should do what they do. What I have listed below is certainly not exhaustive, but it is a good start on the reason for second chairs.

Here are five *whys* of leading from the second chair.

1. *It advances the mission of the church.* Second-chair leaders who advance the mission of the church lift the ministry of the first chair. The mission of the church is the reason for the second chair to serve the first chair.

   There is no reason for us to exist in the church if not for our mission to reach a spiritually lost world with the gospel. If that is true, then it only makes sense second-chair leaders who advance that mission actually advance the ministry of the first chair in doing so. Second-chair leaders who lose focus of the mission of the church will only experience short-term successes in their own ministry and will shortchange the efforts of the senior leader in a dramatic way. Those who choose to advance the mission will find great success as, by their actions, they lift the first chair's leadership.

   When second-chair leaders are actively advancing the mission of the church, they are multiplying the effectiveness of the first-chair leader. Second-chair leaders lift first-chair leaders because it advances the mission of the church. Since the beginning of time, there has been no other cause greater on earth.

2. *It is simply wise and smart to do so.* Second-chair leaders who seek wisdom and think smart will advance the mission of the church and the lead pastor. Foolish and poorly thought-out efforts only serve to diminish the mission and the efforts of the first chair.

   Wise or foolish. Smart or not so smart. It's your choice. Think about it. If you could have all the wisdom and all the smarts in the world, wouldn't it be of high value to bring that to bear in lifting your lead pastor? If you do so, can you imagine what could be the long-range implication to the ministry? Think of how your individual ministry would advance. Do all you can to stay on your face before God in seeking his wisdom. Then combine that with the intellect he gave you to make good decisions.

3. *It makes the second chair better.* A better second chair makes for the best first chair. A better you is better equipped to do the *hows* of second-chair leadership.

   This strikes at one of the centerpiece themes of major ministries. Daily, continual improvement in your ministry makes for a better you. No matter how well you have served the lead pastor yesterday or last week or month, you can always do it better. Being better takes time, and it takes work. It does not necessarily come easy. But being better makes for the best first chair. Our mission is too important for our first chair to not be the best. So it is important you do all you can to enrich and enhance your own person and ministry development. When you do, the ministry wins.

4. *It eventually comes home to roost.* Second-chair leaders will find it tough sledding in their own ministries if they do not lift the hands of the first-chair leader. What you sow you reap.

    We all have heard and experienced this principle. Galatians 6:7b comes to mind: "… for whatever one sows, that will he also reap" (ESV). It follows up with "Do not be weary in doing good." This can certainly be applied to all we do as second-chair leaders. Sow good and reap good. Sow discord or disunity, and guess what? It will be right back at you.

    If you truly want to see the mission of the church you serve advanced and the first-chair leader you serve able to cast vision and grow the church, you will be well advised to sow those things that will produce to that end. Your ministry will flourish when the overall ministry flourishes. If you sow things that diminish the ministry of the church as a whole, your individual ministry will eventually experience the same diminishing.

5. *It is unifying.* Second-chair leaders want to bring unity to the body and to the first chair's team. Psalm 133:1 says, "Behold, how good and pleasant it is when brothers dwell in unity!" (ESV).

When you are confronted with anything that smacks of disunity, it is your role as a second-chair leader to nip it in the bud immediately. As a second-chair leader, you may have a disproportionate amount of power in directing the words and actions of others that could be disunifying to those unifying. Always seek for ways in which that psalm can be said of all aspects of the ministry in the church you serve. When you do so, the lead pastor will experience more success, and the Lord will receive more glory than when disunity exists in the body.

These five reasons for a second chair to lead with the first chair in mind will do more to advance the work and ministry of that first-chair leader than most anything else. The mission of the church is too great to do anything less.

Be wise and be smart. Be better as a second-chair leader. Keep in mind if you do not follow these admonitions, it will come home to roost on you. Be unifying, and above all else, advance the mission of the church.

When you do, the church and the kingdom win!

CHAPTER 24

FIVE WAYS TO HELP YOUR STAFF PASTOR GROW IN EFFECTIVENESS

While Reid was writing the book on how to serve in the second-chair role, Pastor Caleb had another strong staff member in his youth pastor. However, he had three other pastors that were sorely lacking in their effectiveness. Pastor Emery Hardy was a pied piper with students. They followed her lead and were truly becoming some of the finest disciples the church was developing. Caleb felt he was doing a good job in developing Reid and Emery, and he was doing the same things with the other three. However, the lack of performance by those three was nagging at him.

As he and I discussed what was working right and what wasn't in terms of his development process with the team, we identified five simple ways he could improve. He certainly needed to understand just because Emery and Reid were on the mark did not mean the music, children's, and adults pastor were going to be. Caleb needed to make some clear process choices as he attempted to grow his team.

For lead pastors in multiple staff settings, the issue of helping other staff members grow in effectiveness can make or break the lead pastor's ability to truly move the church to the highest possible levels in growth. Many lead pastors are blessed to have fine teams around them. Others are not so fortunate. For all lead pastors, however, helping the people God has given them grow is a forefront issue.

I am operating from the perspective that virtually all staff pastors want to do well in their work and service to the lead pastor and to the church. Some may look like lazy bones from time to time, but you have the opportunity to mold them into something that can be very useful for the kingdom. How can that be done?

While each staff member will respond uniquely to different initiatives and approaches from you, collectively, they can do more than you can imagine when you lead them well. Here are just a few thoughts to that end.

1. *Pray for them.* This can seem so simple, but it is too often overlooked. Consider this. If you had the best talent money could buy at your staff table and they operated without an anointing of God on their lives, what part of 100 percent do you think they could operate? Pick any number. Whatever it is, it will be less than 100 percent, and why would you ever want that? You need to pray regularly and fervently for every staff member on your team. They could do a lot of good things but never 100 percent. Never assume because they came to you with stellar credentials from their previous ministry or since they excelled while at Bible college or seminary they have all they need to be successful in God's eyes at your church. It is just not true. A faithful leader prays. You should do nothing less.

2. *Teach them to think.* One of the great leadership books of recent years is Dr. Steven Sample's *The Contrarian's Guide to Leadership.* In it he develops the concept of not thinking like everyone else thinks, thinking contrary to the norm. In your case, teach your staff pastor to think of things not as they are but as they can be. For example, if the average children's pastor thinks to the extent of having a children's ministry to 200, then to not think differently will limit the ability of the children's ministry to grow beyond 200. You know what that mentality will do to the overall growth of the church. Encourage them to think differently. Frankly, *Contrarian* is an outstanding book for your own leadership as well.

3. *Help them think beyond a set of tasks.* Some staff members, often younger ones, will look at a ministry description and see it as a task list. If they can accomplish their list, then they have done their job. The problem with this is in ministry, you can never effectively list all that needs to be done. Further, when a staff member thinks in these terms, they are thinking like a hireling rather than a pastor/leader. It is your job to help them understand their need to think in terms of ministry mission and then to ask how they can do more toward that mission than to simply crunch out a task list. In other words, teach them to think like a pastor/leader.

4. *Invest in them.* Anyone in business knows if you expect a return, you must make an investment. The single largest line item in any church budget is generally staff compensation. That begs the question, "Why would you not invest in something you are spending so much money on to be successful?" As the lead pastor, you must carry the banner of investing in your staff pastors. Sometimes that means arguing for conference and networking opportunities for your team. Consider the staff member's need and invest to that end. At the other end, where the staff member may be strong, look for investments that will make them even stronger. Just because a staff member has phenomenal gifts and talents in one specific area does not mean they cannot grow further in that area. Ask any athlete who breaks a world record if they then stop trying to break world records. Never. Invest, invest, and then invest again.

5. *Set reputations for them.* This one is huge. Think small of your staff, and you are guaranteed to get small. Think big of them, and you might just get it! Your opinion of your staff member is far greater to them than theirs is to you. Make sense? When the person at the top of the ministry has a sense of greatness for a staff pastor, more often than not the staff pastor will rise to the level of expectation. Set high reputations for your staff pastors. Communicate the same to them.

You have nothing to lose, and the church has a tremendous amount to gain.

At the end of the day, you can lead your staff pastors to be more than they are today. Most want you to do so. Step up and make application of the points listed above. Do not delay. Your mission is too important to let this slide. Your effectiveness in accomplishing what God wants you to do is in large part tied to your success in getting this done.

Staff pastors are a gift from the Lord. Treat them as such and then help them grow into the men and women God wants them to be.

CHAPTER 25

MOTIVATING A PASTORAL STAFF FOR EFFECTIVE MINISTRY

I love to read!

Over the last three years, besides the Bible, I have purposed to read one particular book each year. That book is the classic by Dale Carnegie, *How to Win Friends and Influence People*, written in 1937. Every time I read it, I come away motivated to, guess what? Win friends and influence people. For purposes of this chapter I've included much of Carnegie's outlines and fleshed them out for leadership and development of pastoral teams.

Let's talk about what it takes to motivate your pastoral staff to the highest levels of performance. I know it sounds a bit odd for us to think in terms motivating people who should, by their calling, have the highest of motivation. Welcome to dealing with the real world of people. To state the obvious, staff pastors are people and healthy motivation is necessary and good.

So where do we start? Here are the three primary things to do when motivating a pastoral staff to effective ministry:

1. *Pray.* For those of us who believe we are so good we can simply set our charm in motion to

achieve God-sized plans for the church, we are sorely mistaken. It is critical we pray.

2. *Motivate to mission.* Everything we do must drive to mission. We own the greatest mission on the planet. The eternal consequences of the church's success are enormous. When we challenge our staff pastors to that mission, the church and the kingdom win.

3. *Honor your co-laborer.* We must at all times speak in honoring terms to those called to serve with us. Never approach motivation in a condescending way. Do that, and you will have short-term gains and long-term disasters. Honor them, esteem them, challenge them, and watch God motivate them!

After these primaries are in place, we need to give introspection as to why we motivate. Here are nine questions I ask myself as a church leader regarding staff motivation:

1. *Do I really down deep understand the person to whom I am speaking?* Believe positive, not negative. Truly seek to know and understand. Think of the five people closest to you. Are any of them lazy, unconcerned, or unmotivated? Likely not. Why not? Because you *know* them. Even those whose performance level is lower than yours, as you know and understand them, can be challenged to be better. You must purpose to do just that.

2. *Do I want that person to succeed?* This should be a given, but do you understand the success of the pastoral staff member is a direct contributor to your success as the lead pastor? Call it the "trickle up" concept. You are only as good as those you bring around you. Desire success for your subordinates, and success will be yours.

3. *Do those I lead believe in our mission?* Do your pastors believe to the level you believe? If they do, you are on target to a winning completion of mission. If they do not, you are behind the 8-ball. It is far too easy for subordinates of the lead pastor to become comfortable in their belief of mission. When that happens, a lid is placed on performance. It is your role to lift that lid, inculcate belief in mission to your pastors, and watch performance increase as a result.

4. *Is that to which I am trying to motivate behavior worth doing?* In short, does the church have the goods? Is whatever you are trying to get them to do worth it? You can do all you want in motivation, but if the church you serve does not live up to its mission, it will all be for naught. Figuratively, people are not going to give their life for a bag of potato chips. In the real world, try motivating your staff to the highest performance levels and then going into the pulpit to preach unprepared and watch what happens. You need to evaluate all aspects of church to make sure

you are motivating behaviors worthy of your end product.

5. *Am I sincere?* Unfortunately in church culture, sincerity is sometimes a scarcity. Dig deep within yourself to get the truth. Generally, we are the last to know. Those around you already know.

6. *Do I understand what interests the other person?* When I can understand what interests my co-laborer, I can motivate to that end. The sports-oriented youth pastor will respond differently than the music-oriented children's pastor. Learn these differences, and you will find an increased desire to perform at higher levels.

7. *Am I sincere in making the staff member feel important?* Look directly into the eyes of the other person. Don't overpower, but look and listen. Do not be distracted by people or activity around you. The person must feel as if he or she is the most important thing in the world to you at that moment. There are those who demonstrate a phenomenal ability to make you believe you are their best friend. In the moment of that conversation, to that person, there should be nothing more important to you than them. Go and do likewise!

8. *Do I encourage staff members to talk about themselves?* It is a trade secret of the best motivators. Get other people talking about themselves. When you get a staff member pouring out things about himself, it will not

be long before he begins to believe you care. Hopefully, you are sincere, and you do care. When that happens, an allegiance to you builds, and in turn, the desire to please you jumps exponentially.

9. *Do I appropriately use the sweetest and most important sound to the staff pastor's ear—their name?* My name is music to my ears, and so is yours to yours. Always use your staff members' names when talking and challenging them to higher heights. They love their name. Use it appropriately and with sincerity, and you will see amazing performance improvements.

There comes a time in motivating your staff you need to step up and be the leader. A leader's job often includes motivating staff pastors in their attitudes and behaviors. Carnegie lays out six components of motivating others. As noted earlier I have couched each point in language specific to motivating pastoral team members.

1. *Begin with praise and honest appreciation.* In every occasion of dialogue to motivation, you must praise and sincerely express appreciation for what your staff pastor does for the team and the church. Anything less will yield disappointing results.

2. *Ask questions instead of giving direct orders.* In sales, the person who asks the most questions wins. It is that simple. Always ask questions of

your staff. You validate their opinions when you ask. It does not mean you will buy every answer given, but believe me, you will be miles ahead for having asked.

3. *Praise every improvement. Be lavish in your praise of their achievement to mission.* Fuel the fire of success, large or small. Think about it. No matter how successful you look on the outside, down deep, do you still like it when someone says something good about what you've done? Of course, you do! So why not your staff pastors? Sincere praise leads to increased performance.

4. *Set reputations for them to live up to that are at least currently one step beyond them.* When I played basketball in high school, our starting unit had four outstanding players in their own right—skill players. Then there was me, a distance runner who was skinny, loved the game, and could rebound. At one awards celebration, the coach gave me the Garbage Basketball Award. What was that all about? It was about telling me and the entire team when the ball went loose on the floor, Hardy just seemed to be there. When someone had to lay their body on the line and dive after the ball, it was, guess who? From that moment on, I purposed to be the best garbage basketball player ever. A reputation had been set for me, and I lived up to it. You need to do the same with your pastors. Set reputations!

5. *Make the other person happy about doing the thing you suggest.* The late Zig Ziglar noted "You can have anything in the world you want as long as you can help enough other people get what they want." Your role as the leader is to help your staff member *want* to do what you *want*. When that *want* occurs, everyone wins. When a person wants to do something, they do it with a greater sense of joy than when they simply do what *you* want them to do. Make *them* happy, and you will be happy!

6. *Arouse in the other person an eager want.* You might say, "This all sounds good, but I am not much of a natural in dealing with people, let alone motivating them to success." This one is a major fundamental in motivating people.

We want all our pastors to live for others just as we should. Here is the fact, like it or not: People do not really care about what *you* want. They care about what *they* want. We do not say that to each other, but that is the truth. So why fight it? Be smart. Arouse in the staff member an eager want to achieve what you want, the mission of the church. Do so by doing the following:

- Minimizing any sense of loss the staff member feels may result from *them* achieving what you believe needs to be achieved.
- Maximizing their understanding of the gain *they* will receive as a result of achieving what you believe needs to be achieved.

- Tie understanding of what *they* gain to a practical appreciation of *their* contribution to mission.

Remember, none of this works if you do not pray, motivate to mission, and honor your co-laborer. So do these things and watch God do what only he can do. You will have one motivated staff!

CHAPTER 26

DEALING WITH STAFF PASTORS WHO THINK THEY ARE GOD'S GIFT TO EVERYONE

It certainly was not the fun part of Ric's transition to the Peace Garden State. The team was slow to grab onto what the church would look like as it began to grow. However, there was one team member who was quick to get it and he wasn't shy about letting others know it. Adult Ministries Pastor Patrick was to give guidance to many of the ministry functions and ministries of the church. However, to put it bluntly, Patrick was arrogant. In fact, it went beyond arrogant. Patrick was perceived by almost everyone as feeling he was God's gift to everyone. This was not a pleasant awakening for Ric.

In his previous church, Ric had been used to dealing with wonderful servants who, if not inwardly, certainly on the outside carried an air of humility. Most were truly humble. Now he found himself dealing with a self-proclaimed prima donna and, frankly, not seeing a lot of evidence in his performance his self-proclamation was warranted. Ric and I needed a game plan for dealing with Patrick.

Maybe you've faced this too. You and Ric are not the first lead pastors to have to deal with that one. I know for those who are not lead pastors, you might be saying to yourself, "What about the lead pastor who thinks they are God's gift to everyone?" I suggest we try to minimize the rhetoric and take a look at an issue that is not new to mankind—pride and arrogance.

The stakes are high on this one. Doing it wrong has multiplied negative implications for the lead pastor, staff member, and the church. So let's start at the beginning of the food chain.

As the senior leader, it is imperative you operate with a sense of confidence in your own leadership. You do not have to be arrogant, but you must be confident. Your confident nonarrogance must be perceived accurately by your team collectively and each person individually. I know this is a difficult issue for a number of pastors. I can only suggest you seek to gain confidence from the Lord in your role as the senior leader of your great church.

Once that is in place, it is important each staff member feel validated in their role on the team. On the front end of any hire, this is easy. Down the line, it gets tougher. You want to do all you can to strengthen confidence in staff members. The last thing you need is to do things to diminish confidence in others.

The real world of church, unfortunately, does have those overly confident, arrogant staff members who truly believe the ministry will cease to function effectively if they do not show their stuff. Believe me, when you get stuck with one of these folks, it is not anywhere near fun.

Here are the warning signs:

1. The staff member begins to experience great success.

2. Accolades come their way, and rather than deflect them to others, they begin to "humbly" accept them.

3. Then the "humbly" leaves. They just flat-out believe their press clippings.

4. They draw a fan club around them with people who are more committed to the staff member than they are to the mission of the church. Be clear on this. This is not about lay workers *liking* the staff person more than you. It is about the staff member becoming more *important* than the mission and more *important* than the lead pastor.

5. In communication with you, there is a sense they are the reason for the growth or good things that happen at the church. I must note, be careful here. Do not allow your own insecurities to color a "sense."

6. The staff member begins to lord it over the head of the lead pastor that they are simply irreplaceable and that the lead pastor cannot afford to lose them.

Stop right there!
The minute you believe that, you are toast. No one is irreplaceable. Period. I do not care how good the person is; if they begin to put you in a corner with a confidence you cannot do the drill without them, you must stop. It generally will not be spoken, but if it is there, you need to stop now! Examine how in the world you let the

issue get that far and then pray. You should have been praying in the first place. But here you are.

You must go back to your own sense of confidence. It will likely take a good amount of time to gain back the confidence you need to stand up to the staff member, but it must be done. Your confidence is from God. Rest in that.

Here are steps for you to take:

1. Do not react in haste.

2. Gather your wits about yourself.

3. Pray for God to guide you in the reclaiming of appropriate leadership station in the mind of the staff member.

4. Arrange to meet with the staff member to discuss your observation and get their feedback. Understand a variety of responses can come from that meeting, including "You're making something out of nothing" to "These people love what I am doing and wish you [the lead pastor] would get with it." Do not buy either of them.

5. With appropriate strength and confidence, communicate your observations.

6. Give clear communication of how the future will look in terms of your relationship with the staff member and how you want them to conduct themselves.

7. Make sure they understand that any communication of your private discussions to people

other than the two of you will be grounds for serious discipline and potential dismissal.

8. Understand because the issue has gone this far, you may need to part ways with the staff member and take the corresponding hits from their "fan club" and the church at large. I do not know how to sugarcoat this. This is the reality.

9. Follow through with what you say.

Please, please, please do not allow yourself to get in this boat. Invoke and command the leadership principle of "You can follow me as I follow Christ." Never be arrogant in your own right. Always be confident in the Lord's hand of leadership on you. Despite how you feel, you are the leader. Act like it.

For those staff members who have read this far and feel I have been one-sided, go back up to the third paragraph and make application of those words for yourself. God has gifted you with leadership as well. Just be sure you are putting confident humility under the umbrella of your senior leader in your own leadership.

CHAPTER 27

WHAT I WISH MY STAFF MEMBERS UNDERSTOOD

Greg never did implement the pay-on-commission package as we wrote it for staff members. However, he was constantly trying to communicate higher levels of performance to his already-good staff. He was not a slave driver, but he worked hard, and he expected the same from others.

One of Greg's challenges was getting his staff to understand the pressures of the lead pastor position without them actually walking in those shoes, a challenge at the least. Greg was not unlike many pastors who regularly try to be all things to all staff members and frequently succeed at being none to any. If you find yourself in that role, you might consider this approach to your dilemma.

Associate pastors regularly try to figure out what their lead pastor thinks and why. They generally want to satisfy the lead pastor but often cannot figure out how to do so. Sometimes, when they really find out what the lead pastor wants, the staff member simply does not want to operate at that level.

For the lead pastor, as the senior spiritual leader of the church, it is absolutely critical those staff members who serve with them understand what they think and why. They must be in complete alignment with the direction the Lord has given the leader. Open discussion, healthy disagreement, and thoughtful reflection are hallmarks of the highest-quality staffs.

Lead pastors have an obligation to communicate what they feel the staff should know about church and leadership. Further, lead pastors must hold the staff accountable to the content of those communications.

Staff pastors have an obligation to move into total alignment with the philosophy of the lead pastor. They must understand chain of command and conduct themselves accordingly.

Here are some bullet points for staff members to understand how some lead pastors view staff issues.

1. I do not owe them a job, nor does the church board.

2. It is a privilege to work at the church.

3. I value education, but a BA, MA, MS, D.Min, or PhD does not qualify the staff member to be a spiritual leader.

4. Staff members should not overvalue themselves.

5. I am a caring, compassionate leader, *and* I expect hard work out of my staff members.

6. Although I look forward to interacting personally with staff, I will not do so equally with all people.

7. I will likely not be every staff member's pal.

8. I have more weaknesses than I care to admit. I am working on those as God directs me.

However, my weaknesses are not an excuse for you succumbing to yours.

9. I am looking for people who understand mission. Those that do will help me share the gospel of Jesus Christ with those who do not know him. I am looking for people who know how to lead others to Christ and make disciples.

10. I am not against trends. I am for retrending all the time. However, I am against chasing every bunny trail the church world offers up. I want a staff that sticks to the knitting.

11. The mission of the church consumes me. The mission of the whole overrides any desire I might have to develop a staff member individually. They do not have to be mutually exclusive, but they can be.

12. The buck stops with me. Hence, anything done that reflects negatively on the church, the staff member, or me is going to catch my attention and my correction.

13. Staff members need to regularly keep me informed. I do not have to know every detail about everything, but keep the *Reader's Digest* version in front of me.

14. The staff member needs to keep the spirit of unity. If the leaders of the church are not united, then the body will not be.

15. I am the leader. I am not a dictator, but the Lord has charged me with being the leader. The staff member needs to be in alignment with my leadership.

16. The staff member needs to be in alignment with the direction of the church as a whole. While I'm interested in the staff member's vision, it must align with where we are going overall.

17. We have a church to grow. Although I want to help each staff member grow and develop individually, I expect a good amount of that growth and development to occur as a result of their personal initiative to enable growth to happen.

18. I am looking for hard-charging self-starters.

19. I will be fervent in prayer, and I expect the staff member to be likewise.

In short, a church led by a lead pastor called by God to guide that local body of believers is blessed to have a good thing. That same church infused with staff leadership that understands the way a lead pastor thinks and leads is blessed exponentially.

A lead pastor asks, "What do I wish my staff members understood"? Answer: All of the above!

SECTION 6
CRITICISM

CHAPTER 28
SIX THINGS I LEARNED ABOUT CRITICISM

A year or so ago, I had one of those moments when a critic showed up on the other end of my phone. I had known this pastor (the critic) for a number of years and considered him a good, casual friend. Still do. Although I have to tell you that to be this guy's friend took work. He didn't have many friends, and I wanted to be at least one of the few. We lived in separate cities and talked maybe once a year if that. That was about it.

This particular day, he initiated the call, which was not the norm. Always putting on the schmooze, I did the what's up routine with him. He proceeded to point out to me how I had missed something of great importance in one of my instructional articles for churches and pastors. It was a huge gap I had missed when writing the article. Huge! A complete blind spot. I thanked him for catching it and told him I would correct it right away. End of part 1.

Then the problem came, part 2. He proceeded to launch into a litany of all sorts of things that had gone wrong with a church of which we both were familiar. I had served this church in the past and unrelated to any of the service I had provided it had subsequently fallen on hard times. This pastor/friend/critic felt they would not be in such a mess if only they had just done this and that. In doing so, he exposed to me how he had engaged in gossip, had his facts in total disarray, and, in general, was absolutely clueless of what he was talking about. He really ticked me off. Besides , while listening to his part 2 tirade, I was losing precious time getting back to my website to correct the part 1 error he had correctly noted.

I had trouble shaking this conversation. I wanted to delete him from my e-mail list. I asked God why in the world this guy was in my life. Why could he not just have called me with part 1 and left it with that? Maybe he could have been kind and diplomatic in his criticism. I would have been forever grateful. As it turned out, my mind could not shake that encounter.

This kind of criticism comes to pastors far more than we would like. The fact is we are forced to deal with this stuff at inopportune times. As well, we feel as if we waste valuable minutes trying to determine what is right and what is not.

What are some thoughts on criticism that can help pastors navigate these unpleasantries? Here are six things I noted on my encounter described above:

1. *The criticism came from a friend/acquaintance who was not close to me.* What does this tell us? Everyone is a potential critic. Those we do not think of as helpful critics *are* sometimes helpful.

2. *My closest friends and people who knew me well did not call with the criticism.* What does this tell us? Oftentimes, the people closest to us, those we respect the most, do not communicate our failures to us. We wish they did because we trust them. But frequently they don't.

3. *The criticism came from someone who arguably had trouble saying things in a diplomatic manner.* What does this tell us? God never promises us pretty critics. Some carriers of truth can be really messy in saying what they need to say. Frequently critics are deplorable diplomats.

4. *Multiple criticisms came at the same time.* What does this tell us? Sometimes you have to decipher what is valid and what is not. Critics often use the machine-gun approach of communication. They fire away criticisms without regard for what might be valid and what might not be. Truth and error can come from the same mouth.

5. *The criticism messed with my head.* What does this tell us? You're human. You have to aggressively give this to God and seek his perspective on your response. The level of aggressiveness depends on your emotional disposition. You need to know yourself well before the criticism hits.

6. *The critic was wrong on most but not all counts.* What does this tell us? The critic is human. It's easy to say but much harder to live in the practical application of its truth in our minds. In fact, you might be right more than the critic gives you credit for.

When a pastor can rightly discern criticism as truth or error, they are on the right road to being better at all they do. Always be open to what others have to say, realizing it frequently comes in messy packages. At the same time, make sure you know yourself and how you respond. Deal with criticism as quickly as possible and then get on about the business of being the best pastor you can be, receiving the truth and ditching the error.

CHAPTER 29

NINE THOUGHTS ON DEALING WITH FOUNDED CRITICISM

After Pastor Jerry moved out from the cloud of dust created by the unfounded critics in his life, he had the unenviable task of now discerning which critics were founded in their criticism. He and I talked about the pain he and his wife, Caitlin had experienced with the clueless ones. He was wise, however, in stating to me he never wanted to be blind to what others who truly cared about him and the church saw in his life. A wise man, indeed.

Part of Jerry's challenge was helping his wife appreciate legitimate critics. Her pain ran deep from the unfounded criticism. Jerry learned early on criticism aimed at him is also received by his wife. To discern which was founded and which was not and to help her in that understanding was not an easy task or one for the faint of heart.

You probably join Jerry and me in saying, "I just hate it when my critic is right." You work hard to do everything right, and then from out in left field, a critic makes a statement, and he or she is right. If you're like me, you wish all the correct-observation criticisms would come in nice, neat packages. Generally, they don't.

For starters, let's think about criticism itself. What does it look like? Why does it happen? How can we discern its value to our lives and ministries?

In an attempt to separate founded from unfounded criticisms, some pastors use a fourfold approach in that determination.

1. *Source—when you consider the source, it drives to motivation.* Did it come from someone who loves you deeply and is motivated to your betterment? Did it come from an off-the-wall person who really knows you very little and could care less about your betterment?

2. *Evaluate—always ask questions.* The person who asks the most questions wins. Take time to search out. Ask others to weigh in and then listen to those who know and love you. You need honesty with them and with yourself.

3. *Value—place value on the source.* If it is a long-term member who loves you deeply, that is one thing—high value. If it is the guy who just showed up last week and decides to tell you how to preach, that is something else—low value.

4. *Response—sometimes your response is to do nothing.* That is a response. After you evaluate the criticism, the value you place on the source directs your response. Low value, low response. High value, high response.

When you face the reality a founded criticism has come your way, here are some thoughts on processing that criticism.

1. *Do an attitude check.* This is necessary both for your own self-assessment and your evaluation of the critic and the criticism. Determine whether the critic is still able to remain under your spiritual covering and that of the church. Is their attitude right and pure?

2. *Do not become defensive.* Your human nature says to buck the critic. Spiritual wisdom says to listen attentively and keep your defenses lowered. You may need to hear what the critic says, regardless whether they say it in a nice, neat way or not.

3. *Validate the criticism with trusted confidants.* Always have people near you who can reflect on the criticism with you. They need to give you honest feedback.

4. *Demonstrate humility.* God did not call you to be the infallible know-it-all. Take your medicine. Be humble.

5. *Don't make excuses.* When you're wrong, you're wrong. Face up to it. Own it!

6. *Empathize with the critic.* When a critic is correct, always empathize with them. Even when your defense mechanisms want to justify some part of the action for which you are being criticized, always defer to empathizing.

7. *Acknowledge founded criticism sometimes comes in a messy package.* Forget the messiness. Listen up. When it's right, it's right.

8. *The ministry is first and foremost.* Be prayerful and confident in all you do. Do what God wants you to do. Be who he wants you to be. Let good criticism help you to that end.

9. *Please God.* Remember that to please God is pre-eminent.

Finally, be aware criticism takes different forms in the different seasons of the church. During times of a lot of change, the noise gets louder and louder. In times of little change, criticism may be minimal. Sometimes it feels like the attacks are more personal. They might be. At all times, however, recognize the season you are in and respond accordingly.

Do you ever feel like you are suffering unduly? Of course, you do. But as you receive the unpleasantness of criticism that seems unfair, you must know there are flickers of truth in many of those criticisms. It's life. It's ministry. Whether we like it or not, it's good.

CHAPTER 30

TEN THOUGHTS ON DEALING WITH CRITICS WHO ARE ABSOLUTELY CLUELESS

Ever dealt with someone who was absolutely clueless? I have, and so have a bunch of other pastors. In Jerry and Caitlin's case, you would have thought after having been there over twenty years in the lead pastor role, cluelessness would have evaporated from their suburban Cleveland church. Not so. They seemed to be alive and well and more vocal than in the past.

On one trip, the three of us spent an entire afternoon and evening in their kitchen and on their deck trying to negotiate an understanding of how some critics could be so far off base and be spiritual about it at the same time. Most of what we were dealing with at the time had no basis in reason. It defied logic. Nonetheless, it was real, and we had to figure out how to deal with it, live with it, or dismiss. Maybe all of the above.

If you are like most lead pastors, criticism comes with the territory. More often than not, the criticism is unfounded. However, because many of us are people pleasers, we take too much of this to heart, and it makes a mess of our heads. Young pastors are particularly susceptible to these criticisms. How you navigate criticism makes all the difference in the world.

Before we go too far, let me make a few observations relative to protecting yourself from clueless critics.

1. Never read anonymous letters. These people are gutless wonders that deserve no response. If you have staff, have them pitch the letter and not tell you it arrived. Instruct them not to read it either.

2. Timing. Never check e-mails on Saturday night or Sunday morning. Satan knows when to yank your chain to throw you off kilter.

3. If you have multiple services, be careful who you talk to between services. Keep protection up against chronic critics.

4. Be aware of energy vampires who seek to drain everything out of you. Do all you can to build a hedge of protection around yourself and against these people.

For criticism to be of value, it must align itself with the mission of the church. Unfounded criticism does not. Discerning whether it does or does not is crucial. To that end, unfounded criticisms can generally be put in four different categories.

1. *Comments—this is when something is said off the cuff.* It is nothing more than a comment. Don't give it the time of day. Move on.

2. *Confusion—this is where the critic needs more or better information.* This is the pastor's opportunity to clarify. Acknowledge you may have done something to create a wrong impression in the critic's mind. If you have, fix it.

3. *Crisis—when people go through crisis, sometimes they criticize as an emotional expression.* This is how they ask for help. At this juncture, the pastor needs to care.

4. *Culture—here the criticism is not in alignment with mission.* The criticism simply does not fit with the culture. You must deal with the critic directly. Cast a good, strong vision. The stronger the process you have in place, the less the cultural criticism.

We like to think when a founded criticism comes our way, we are ready to hear and be better. It may not be fun, but we do *want* to know. However, when a clueless critic presents their criticism, how do we handle that? Here are some thoughts on processing unfounded criticism—the good, the bad, and the ugly.

1. *Do a pre-emptive strike.* Never wait for critics to show up. Trust me, they're out there. While planning for the best, always prepare for the worse when it comes to these people. Get ahead of the criticism. When you sense something may be coming your way, get ahead of it. As Barney Fife famously noted, "Nip it! Nip it in the bud!"

2. *Consider the source.* When the person is someone new to you or the church and they have no history of support of the ministry, I would place a low value on their criticism. Still listen but do not go far with it.

3. *Remember, it's a small minority.* Usually the criticism comes from a small minority, grumbling and complaining. They do so stating a lot of people are upset at what you are doing. This small minority seldom come to you directly with their criticism.

4. *Have in place a strong leadership team.* A strong board can be invaluable when a ruckus resulting in criticism starts in the church. This is where being pre-emptive comes in to play as well.

5. *Attempt to correct perception.* A critic may simply have wrong information. When you present accurate information to them. sometimes they will listen. Sometimes not. Be prepared for either.

6. *Don't be drawn in to typical debates.* Frequently the critic wants to engage you in a deep theological debate in which many have engaged in the past. While you are the spiritual leader of the church, please know there will be critics of your doctrinal stances and interpretations of Scripture. Communicate to the one who disagrees with you most vehemently that folks a lot smarter than the two of you added together have debated these issues and never come to agreement. Stake out your position without engaging in a debate that will never be won with critics whose criticism is unfounded.

7. *Sometimes call the critic on unfounded criticism.* Do not roll over like a puppy dog. When criticism comes your way, there are times to call the critic on the error of their criticism. There are times when they need to know which end is up and that their pastor is not some wimp they can attack at will. Do not go looking for a fight, but also don't roll over when the critic is wrong.

8. *Or maybe it may not be worth the fight.* When unfounded criticism comes your way, do all you can to not give it emotional energy. That's easy to write about and not near as easy to do. Remember, it is the Lord who brings vindication.

9. *Maintain your testimony.* Reacting poorly to even the most off-the-wall criticism is not worth it. Your testimony of what God has done in your life is far more valuable. Never forfeit that.

10. *Apply 1 Peter 5:7*: "Humble yourselves, therefore, under the mighty hand of God so that at the proper time he may exalt you, casting all your anxieties on him, because he cares for you" (ESV).

At the end of the day, you need to have your head screwed on straight with these critics. They are truly clueless, and they can mess with your head. Do not let that happen. Be gracious and kind. Be forthright and clear. Pray for the critic and do not do so in a condescending way. Keep your energies channeled to those things that drive to mission.

For the congregation you serve, teach and preach on how to respond to criticism, founded and unfounded. Point them to books like *The Bait of Satan* by John Bevere where the author describes how Satan lures believers to take up an offense, one of his most deceptive snares. Help them understand the enemy's effort in creating turmoil through criticism and offense.

Even the best leaders in scripture, Old Testament and New Testament, had their clueless critics. Jesus certainly had his. You have yours. Give the care of these criticisms to the Lord and watch him move your ministry forward despite unfounded criticism. In all things, be secure in who God called you to be. It sounds trite, but when you do, God takes care of the clueless critics and their unfounded criticisms.

Quit piddling around with the clueless critics. You've got stuff to do. Get busy!

With criticism, it is all about perspective. By now you have six friends giving you perspective. Pastors Rick, Lou, Jerry, Greg, Caleb and I all say the same thing. Our advice to you is to listen to your critics, discern, and then go with God's perspective. You'll be glad you did!

THE HARDY GROUP

PASTORAL LEADERSHIP CONSULTING

At The Hardy Group we believe church doesn't have to be what it always has been, and we believe you can lead at an entirely new level.

"SO WHAT'S IN IT FOR ME?" YOU ASK.

- ◆ Advanced ability to think larger than you are currently.
- ◆ Increased number of people accepting Christ, getting baptized and discipled.
- ◆ Enhanced confidence in growing and reinventing your leadership.
- ◆ Accessibility to 30 years of mega church experience now at your fingertips.
- ◆ Definition and fulfillment of your #1 and #2 priorities, whatever they are.

IT CAN HAPPEN. LET'S TALK TODAY.

CALL OR TEXT (417) 576-5492
OR EMAIL DHARDY@THEHARDYGROUP.ORG
WWW.THEHARDYGROUP.ORG

VIDEO CONSULTING NETWORKS
(FOR CHURCHES UP TO 500 IN SIZE)

The five-member Video Consulting Networks connect you with the value of The Hardy Group along with other pastors striving to break the 500 barrier like the one ahead for you. Join in the monthly video connections interacting with Dick and four other pastors just like you, all trying to be better in leading their churches. For more information, click on Video Consulting at www.thehardygroup.org.

E-NEWSLETTER RESOURCE UPDATES

Every two to three weeks The Hardy Group releases new articles, book reviews, podcasts and church related documents practical to where you live in the local church. We would love to have you as part of our pastoral resource family. It is a free subscription in the upper right hand corner at www.thehardygroup.org.

The Hardy Group
1105 W. Woodbine St
Springfield, MO 65803
dhardy@thehardygroup.org
417-576-5492